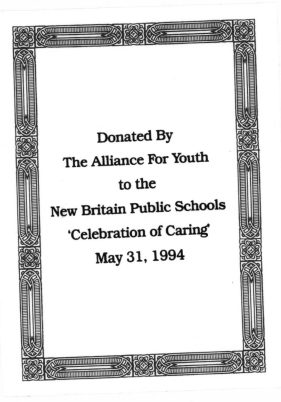

AFGHANISTAN
FIGHTING FOR FREEDOM

DISCOVERING our HERITAGE

by Mir Tamim Ansary

dP| DILLON PRESS
New York

Maxwell Macmillan Canada
Toronto

Maxwell Macmillan International
New York Oxford Singapore Sydney

Acknowledgments

The publisher would like to thank the following people and organizations for providing photographs: the author, Bob Dar, Domino's Pizza, Rick Ergenbright, Karen Fritz, Oliver Hakenberg, Anne Nowrouz, and Bob Pendleton/ the Committee for a Free Afghanistan.

The author gratefully acknowledges the Afghan Cultural Assistance Foundation, the Center for Afghanistan Studies, the Committee for a Free Afghanistan, Paul Overby, Mark Slobin, Farid Ansary, and the Nowrouz family for assistance in locating photographs and for other valuable information.

Library of Congress Cataloging-in-Publication Data

Ansary, Mir Tamim.
    Afghanistan : fighting for freedom / by Mir Tamim Ansary.
        p. cm. — (Discovering our heritage)
    Summary: A look at the politics, culture, geography, and history of Afghanistan.
    ISBN 0-87518-482-0
    1. Afghanistan—Juvenile literature. [1. Afghanistan.]
    I. Title II. Series.
    DS351.5.A57 1991
    958.1—dc20   91-15648

Dillon Press
Macmillan Publishing Company
866 Third Avenue
New York, NY 10022

Maxwell Macmillan Canada, Inc.
1200 Eglinton Avenue East
Suite 200
Don Mills, Ontario M3C 3N1

Macmillan Publishing Company is part of the Maxwell Communication Group of Companies.

First edition
Printed in the United States of America
10   9   8   7   6   5   4   3   2   1

Contents

Fast Facts about Afghanistan

Official Name: Da Afghanistan Democratik Jamhouriet (in Pushto) or Jamhouriet-i-Democratik-i-Afghanistan (in Dari), both of which mean the Democratic Republic of Afghanistan.

Capital: Kabul.

Location: Central Asia; it borders the Soviet Union to the north, Iran to the west, and Pakistan to the south and east.

Area: Approximately 251,773 square miles (652,090 square kilometers). *Greatest Distances*: north-south —630 miles (1,012 kilometers); east-west—820 miles (1,320 kilometers). *Coastlines*: none; Afghanistan is a landlocked nation.

Elevation: *Highest*: 24,557 feet (7,485 meters) above sea level at Naochak, a mountain peak in the Pamir Mountain Range. *Lowest*: Less than 1,500 feet (500 meters) at the central northern border and in a part of the southwestern desert (Sistan Basin).

Population: 15,885,000 (1990 estimate).

Form of Government: Communist—but much of the country is ruled by local military commanders affiliated with political parties based in Pakistan. *Head of Government*: President, military commanders.

Important Products: Barley, corn, cotton, fruits, nuts, rice, vegetables, wheat, karakul skins, mutton, wool, carpets, lapis lazuli, natural gas, coal.

Basic Unit of Money: Afghani.

Major Languages: Dari, Pushto.

Major Religion: Islam (99 percent).

Flag: The flag of the government in Kabul, the capital of Afghanistan, has three horizontal bands of color: black, red, and green, with a coat of arms representing the National Party. The Mujahideen, a resistance movement that controls more than 80 percent of the country, does not recognize this flag.

National Anthem: *Sorud-i-Melli* ("National Anthem").

Major Holidays: Nowroz—March 21; Eid-i-Ramazan, "Holiday of the Month of Fasting," occurs eleven days earlier each year and lasts three days; Eid-i-Qurban, "Holiday of the Sacrifice," occurs two months after Eid-i-Ramazan.

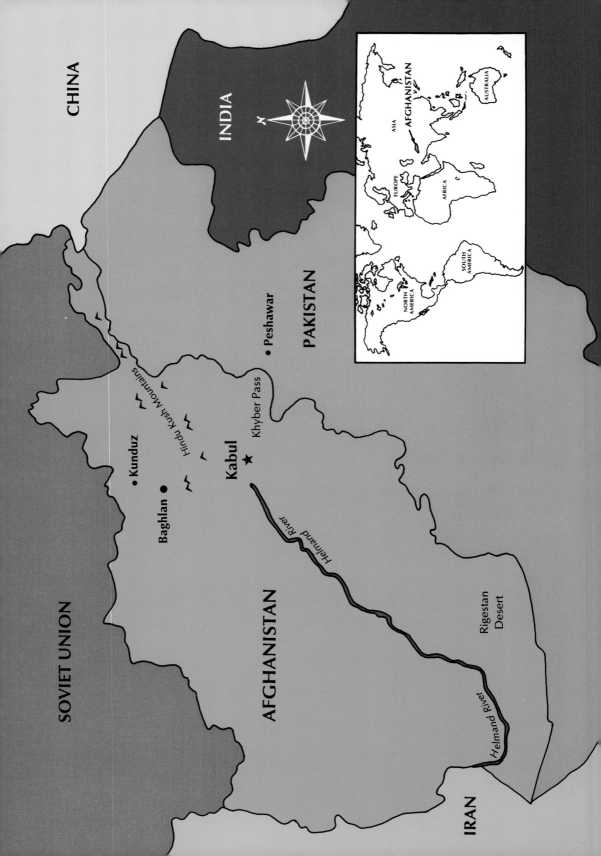

1. A War–Torn Land

Northeast of India, near a city called Peshawar, a dusty highway cuts between bare hills and snakes into the mountains of Afghanistan. The rugged notch between these hills is called the Khyber Pass. Over the years, this spot has been the setting for many a story of romantic danger. Today, the danger remains real enough, but the romance is gone: The Khyber Pass now leads into a land shattered by war.

Government troops patrol the highway from the pass to the capital city of Kabul. Helicopters whir above the road, bringing supplies to forts along the border. Rebel warriors roam the hills that surround the road. In those hills, hundreds of villages stand deserted: Some have been bombed to rubble. Many people have been killed and many more have fled. About five million Afghans now live outside the country as refugees—people driven from their homes by disaster. Countless more live as refugees within the country.

A Rugged Land

To understand the war in Afghanistan, you need to know something of the land and the people. Look at a map of central Asia and you will see that Afghanistan is shaped something like a fist, wedged between the Soviet Union, Iran, and Pakistan. A small "thumb" sticking out from the northeast corner touches the People's Republic of China. No part of the country borders on an ocean or sea. In total area, Afghanistan just about equals the state of Texas.

A branch of the Himalaya Mountains called the Hindu Kush spills into Afghanistan from the east. This mountain range fills up the whole middle of the country with a cluster of peaks. People live in the valleys among the peaks. Most of the valleys are about 5,000 feet (1,523 meters) above sea level. The peaks rise to heights of 17,000 feet (5,181 meters) and more. Snow caps some of these mountains all year round. The highest mountains lie in the Wakhan Corridor, the little "thumb" of land that touches China. Here, even the valleys are 10,000 feet (3,048 meters) above sea level. The highest peaks rise to more than 25,000 feet (7,620 meters).

In northern Afghanistan, the mountains give way to steppes, which are high grassy plains and rolling hills. A low desert fills the southwest corner of the country. Most of the desert is stony and as flat as a lake. The biggest river in Afghanistan, the Helmand, runs through the desert and empties into a marsh on the border between Afghanistan and Iran. South of the Hindu Kush range, Afghanistan has a region of rocky foothills. These hills rise gradually

A small group of mounted men approaches
a rocky pass in mountainous Afghanistan.

A Pushtoon boy in a doorway, with his sister behind him.

from the stony desert of the southwest until they merge into mountains covered with forest in the southeast.

A Hodgepodge of People and Tongues

Many people have swept across Afghanistan over the centuries and each wave has left behind a pool of people. As a result, the people of Afghanistan are even more varied than the landscape.

In the south live the largest group, the Pushtoons, who are also called the Afghans. The country is named

An Uzbek girl holds a younger Uzbek boy.

after them because they have been the ruling group for the last two hundred years or so. From Kabul to the northeastern border (and in all the major cities) live Tajiks, the second largest group. Many of the country's traders and merchants are Tajiks. Pushtoons, Tajiks, and most of the southern tribes are swarthy, black-haired Caucasians. So are the Farsiwans of the southwest. In northern Afghanistan live people of Mongolian stock, such as Turkomans, Uzbeks, and Aimaqs. They have high cheekbones and narrow slanted eyes. Another Mongoloid people, the Hazaras, live in central Afghanistan. Then there is the valley of Panjsher—which means "Five Lions." Here the people apparently descend from the armies of Alexander the Great (mixed with whoever lived there before). These people sometimes have reddish brown hair and freckles. A very few even have blond hair and blue eyes. In the east live the mysterious people of Nuristan. They speak a language related to Basque— which is spoken in an area between France and Spain.

All in all, more than twenty ethnic groups live in Afghanistan. They speak almost that many different languages and dialects. The most common language is *Farsi*, the same language that is spoken in Iran. The dialect spoken in Afghanistan is called *Dari*. The Tajiks, Hazaras, and Farsiwans speak Dari as a first language and many others speak it as a second language. The other main language is *Pushto*, the language of the Pushtoons. Few non-Pushtoons speak Pushto.

The Ones Who Move

About two million Afghans are nomads, which means they live in no one particular place: Instead, they move all the time. They make their living by herding camels and fat-tailed sheep. From their animals, the nomads get milk,

Kochis live in tents and have few belongings, which makes their frequent travels much easier.

meat, lard, and wool, most of which they use themselves and some of which they sell. The nomads keep mostly to open country. But they drift through cities from time to time to sell their products. Afghans call these people *kochis*—"people who move." Kochis move because they must. In Afghanistan, no one place has enough grass and plant life to support a herd of animals for long. If the kochis stayed in one place, their animals would eat up all the food and then starve. So the kochis keep moving. By the time they get back to a particular pasture, the grass and scrub have grown back. Even with a war on, the kochis continue ambling in a huge circle that takes them into Pakistan and back again as the seasons turn. You may see a hundred men, women, and children in a band—but rarely more. They trudge across the barren landscape behind a flock of fat-tailed sheep, with ten or twenty camels plodding along in a string, carrying their tents and supplies.

The Turkoman nomads of northern Afghanistan have red dome-shaped tents. The Pushtoon or Baluchi nomads, who live mostly in the south, have black tents that look like huge bats. Along the edges of a Pushtoon or Baluchi band lope big beasts with heavy shoulders and huge heads. These are the fierce and much-feared kochi dogs.

A thousand years ago, nomads roamed across much of the world. The Plains Indians of North America were nomads. Most European nations started out as nomadic tribes. In central Asia, Turkish and Mongolian nomads carved out some of the biggest empires in history. Today, Afghanistan is one of the few places where large numbers of people still live this rugged, rootless life.

Farming and Handicrafts

Most Afghans live in villages of a few hundred to a few thousand people. They keep some animals but make their living mainly as farmers. Some large landowners live in

A country fort, or qala.

country forts, or *qalas*, surrounded by farmers who work their lands. Afghan farmers grow cotton, fruits, nuts, vegetables, wheat, rice, and other grains. The fruits in this country are especially sweet and varied.

The climate of Afghanistan creates special problems for farmers. Most of the country is cold in winter but hot and dry in summer. Snow melting on the peaks creates thousands of streams, but they thunder down too fast to use in farming. Then comes summer and most of the streams dry up. To solve the water shortage problem, Afghan farmers dig a series of wells in the slopes above their villages. They run the water down to their fields through a tunnel that connects all the wells. This type of well system is called a *kahrez*.

In addition to herding and farming, many Afghan villagers have cottage industries; that is, families work at home and make products for sale. For example, they make embroidered coats from sheepskins and other hand-stitched garments. The northern tribes produce hats from the soft, curly wool of *karakuls*. The Turkoman tribes specialize in making fine carpets, handwoven on simple square looms. These items, along with dried fruits and nuts, have long accounted for most of Afghanistan's exports to other countries.

Before the war, Afghanistan had a few factories, but the number was never large. They included a sugar plant in Baghlan, a cotton company in Kunduz, and a textile mill in Pul-i-Khumri. Now, because of the fighting, most of the factories have shut down. The country's natural resources include natural gas, coal, and *lapis lazuli*, a blue gem. None of these resources is being mined much nowadays except for the lapis lazuli.

Kabul is the capital of Afghanistan and its largest city. Swollen by refugees, it now has over a million people. Kandahar and Herat are the second and third largest. Each had between one and two hundred thousand people before the war.

Kabul is an ancient city—more than two thousand

Modern homes in Kabul, the capital.

years old. It stretches along a narrow valley surrounded by mountains. Two mountain ridges thrust right into the heart of the city, pinching it into an eastern and western half. These ridges are called Koh-i-Sherdarwaza—the "Mountain of the Lion's Door."

The passage between the mountains used to be the entrance to Kabul. You can still see old walls running along each ridge. The walls were built about one thou-

A street scene in Kabul.

sand years ago to keep out enemies. They used to meet in a huge gate—the Lion's Door itself. The Lion's Door crumbled long ago and Kabul spilled through the gate. It spread up and down the valley for miles. What was once the mouth of the city is now its belt. The mud-brick houses of Kabul even crawl up the sides of the mountains.

The Kabul River runs through the middle of the city. New downtown Kabul lies north of a bend in the river. Wide sidewalks line broad paved boulevards. Sleek, boxlike buildings, designed by the Soviets and the West Germans, rise into the air. Here, camels and donkeys must compete for the road with cars, trucks, and buses.

Go east from the river, however, and you enter the dusty maze of Shar-i-Kuhna, or "The Old City." Here the streets form narrow alleys between walled compounds. You will find no street signs here and no addresses on the doors. If you don't know where you are going, you probably have no business here. All of Kabul probably looked like this in the days when the walls were built on Lion's Door Mountain.

Kabul is more than just the capital and the biggest city. It has long been something like the center of a small empire. Each of the many tribal groups living within the borders of Afghanistan considers itself a nation. All these little nations have been ruled by the government in Kabul for about two hundred years. Kabul is to Afghanistan roughly what Rome was to the Roman Empire. In most Afghan cities, one ethnic group tends to dominate. On the streets of Kabul, you see a mixture of all the people. Hazaras have come here from Hazarajat and Pushtoons from the southeast. Tajiks and Uzbeks have come down from the north. People flock to Kabul because it is the center of power, wealth, and commerce.

Afghanistan Today

Kabul and the rest of Afghanistan have been growing apart for a long time. Today, they are really like two different countries. People in Kabul think, live, look, and act differently than most other Afghans. The war has also created a third Afghanistan outside the borders. These are the refugees who live mostly in Pakistan and Iran. At least one out of every four Afghans lives in the refugee camps. Because of this division, Afghanistan no longer has one government. Kabul is controlled by Hizbi Watan (the National Party), a new name for a Communist group that seized power in 1978. The head of the National Party is a man named Najibullah.

Seven "Islamic" parties are fighting the Communist government. All seven have their offices in Pakistan among the refugees. The Islamic parties want Afghanistan to be run according to the religion of Islam. They consider the Communists to be atheists—people who don't believe in God. They also point out that Islam is a whole legal, social, and political system. Therefore, they insist, a country cannot be both Islamic and Communist—and they choose Islamic. The seven Islamic parties have formed their own government headed by a man named Subghatullah Mujaddedi. They claim theirs is the real government of Afghanistan.

Neither government really rules much of Afghanistan. Outside Kabul and the main cities, the only real gover. ners are the local *Mujahideen* commanders. Mujahideen means "those who fight in the cause of Islam." Each commander is a warrior with a group of fighting men.

Most of the Mujahideen are connected to one of the seven Islamic parties in Pakistan. Each one, however, is his own boss and the lord of his own area, big or small. If you know what Europe was like in the Middle Ages, when barons ruled like little kings, you have a pretty good picture of what Afghanistan is like today.

2. The Afghan Way of Life

You cannot discuss what life is like in Afghanistan today without talking about war. People live with the sound of gunfire in the background. Some say this is nothing new. Among their neighbors, the people of Afghanistan have a long-standing reputation as warriors. That's probably because Afghans pride themselves on their independence and have a stern sense of honor. They defend their lands and families fiercely. They avenge insults to their name and honor. Various tribes often have feuds going with one another, and these feuds can last for generations. But let some outsider attack and the tribes unite against the would-be conquerer.

Today's war, however, goes far beyond tribal feuds. It has shattered the country and touched every family. Nonetheless, the picture of the "warlike" Afghan gives a false impression. Beneath the roar of war runs the current of everyday life. In this ancient way of life, manners count for a great deal more than muscles.

Champions of Hospitality

Afghans are very social people. They love to sit around in groups, just chatting and telling stories. People linger

The sound of gunfire is common in this warring country.

for hours in the markets, exchanging views with friends and strangers. Shopkeepers and customers might well drink a few pots of tea together before getting down to bargaining. Even now, in the war-torn countryside, you might possibly come across a group of warriors sitting in a big circle, cleaning their guns and talking.

Above all other virtues, Afghans value hospitality. Most would proudly rank Afghans as the world champions of this virtue. Hospitality goes beyond good manners here: It is more like a sacred code. Travelers in Afghan cities can almost count on getting food, shelter, and other help from strangers on the street —although, of course, in this time of war, there are few idle travelers in Afghan cities.

Every ethnic group has its own version of the code. Pushtoonwali, the code of the Pushtoons, is probably the best-known and most specific. Pushtoonwali involves such points as *melmastia* (being a generous host); *ghayrat* (defending one's honor); *namus* (defending the honor of women); *nanawati* (giving shelter to anyone in need); and *sabat* (being steadfast). Another point in the Pushtoon code, however, is *badal*—avenging blood for blood.

The Pillars of Islam

Almost all Afghans have one thing in common and that one thing is religion. Perhaps ninety-nine out of every one hundred Afghans are followers of Islam. This religion began fourteen centuries ago in Arabia. It was founded by the Prophet Muhammad. Islam teaches that there is only one God—the same God worshiped by Christians and Jews. They believe all the prophets of the Bible, including Jesus, were messengers from God, and that Muhammad was the last messenger. Anyone who embraces this belief in one God and Muhammad as his final messenger is a Musulman, a follower of Islam. (In the West, followers of Islam are usually called Muslims or Moslems.)

Of course, there is much more to being a Muslim than

embracing one belief. Good Muslims live according to the message Muhammad brought. They say certain prayers five times a day. They fast during one month of the year. They visit the Arabian city of Mecca at least once in a lifetime (if they can). They give a certain portion of their wealth to the needy. These duties, along with the belief in one God and in Muhammad as his messenger, are often called the five pillars of Islam.

The first guide to Muslim life is the Holy *Koran*, the book Muhammad presented to the world. Almost every Afghan family has a copy of the Koran wrapped in cloth and placed on a high shelf above all other books. Muhammad himself is the second guide. Because he was chosen as God's messenger, his whole life is considered part of the message. Any question not covered in the Koran can be answered by studying what Muhammad did or said in a similar situation. Even the smallest village has at least one man who has studied both the Koran and the Prophet's life. This man is called a *mullah*.

In the Koran, God is called *Allah*. However, Muslims do not think of Allah as "a God" or "the God of the Muslims." Allah is simply the Arabic word for God—the only God. Afghans often refer to Him by the Dari word *Khudawand*. But they also use Allah in the many Arabic words and phrases woven into daily life. For example, Afghans hardly ever announce a plan without adding *"inshallah"*—which, in Arabic, means "if God wills."

Islam forbids the drinking of alcohol. Therefore, beer, wine, and whiskey cannot be found anywhere in Afghanistan—except in Kabul. Before the war, a number of bars and nightclubs sprang up in the capital, shocking followers of the old ways.

Islam also considers pork unclean and forbids people to eat this meat. Therefore, no one keeps pigs or eats any pork product—not even in Kabul. In fact, Afghans find the very thought disgusting—rather the way you might feel about eating a cockroach.

The rules of Islam make life very different for men and women. Until recently, most Afghans believed that women should not be seen at all by men outside their families. They considered it shameful and immodest. For this reason, most Afghans live in a compound, a dwelling surrounded by a high wall. This wall keeps outsiders from peeking in.

When women leave their compound to go out in public, they make sure to clothe themselves fully from head to foot. At one time, Afghan women had to wear *chadris* in public. A chadri is a pleated bag that goes over a woman's head and comes down to her ankles. A strip of mesh at eye level allows her to look out. A law passed in 1959 abolished chadris, but some women still wear them.

Although Islam does not actually require that women wear chadris, it does have rules about the way people

Women wearing chadris.

should dress. Outside of Kabul, most Afghans conform to these rules. Men and women alike wear baggy pantaloons held up by a drawstring. Over the pantaloons, the women wear a long dress. Men wear a knee-length shirt.

Islam recommends that people keep their heads covered, so most Afghans wear some kind of headgear. Women wear scarves. Men usually wear a skullcap with a turban wrapped around it. A turban is a long strip of cloth. Different tribes tie their turbans in different ways. Some, for example, wear the turban big and puffy; others leave a strip dangling down over their shoulder. Men with

money and a sense of fashion often wear karakul hats
instead of turbans. Karakul hats are shaped like brimless
derbies. They come from the tribes of the north. Another
type of cap has lately gained popularity. This is the *pakol*,
a tan pillbox hat worn by the Mujahideen as a mark of
their resistance to the government. It was the everyday
hat of the people of Nuristan, where the rebellion began.
The Mujahideen wear it as a kind of badge of their
rebellion. Lately, however, even the president they are
fighting sometimes wears a Mujahideen cap in public.

In the city of Kabul, unlike other parts of the country,
many people no longer wear traditional Muslim dress.
They have adopted Western-style clothes—jeans, slacks,
suits, dresses, blouses, and so on. In the provinces almost
all men have mustaches and beards, as recommended by
Islam. In Kabul, a great many men are clean-shaven.

Witty Words, Bright Colors

Afghans love language. Listen to any conversation between friends and you will hear rhymed lines, proverbs,
and quotations from poets. Poetry, in fact, is closely
woven into many aspects of daily life in Afghanistan.
The words to many pop songs are classic poems written
long before the time of Shakespeare. Educated men make
a game of quoting lines from classic works of literature
back and forth. Even people who can't read often know

Afghan women have raised embroidery to a high art. These children wear embroidered hats and clothing.

hundreds of poems by heart. The finest Afghan poet of modern times, Khalilullah Khalili, died recently in Pakistan, where he was living as a refugee. One collection of his poems is called *Matumserai*—"The House of Wailing." These poems mourn the sad fate of Afghanistan. Today, many of the Mujahideen warriors quote his verses as anthems of their struggle.

Islam strictly forbids the worship of idols. This has discouraged many Muslims from painting or carving any images of reality. Afghan artists, therefore, favor abstract work. They use mosaic tiles, for example, to cover

Close-up of a Turkoman rug, showing the elephant-foot pattern.

mosques and shrines with complex patterns. They use calligraphy (decorative handwriting) to create posters with words from the Koran. Most of the art that ordinary Afghans might own are decorated objects. Afghans love color and tend to cover everything they use with ornaments! Nomads decorate their animals, and truck drivers paint their trucks. Afghan women have raised embroidery to a high art, working gold braid, mirrors, colored threads, and other ornaments into the garments they make.

Handicrafts, in fact, are among Afghanistan's best-known exports. The bloodred Turkoman rugs probably top the list. These rugs have a characteristic pattern of eight-sided boxes filled with and surrounded by intricate patterns. Each eight-sided box is called an elephant foot. Good Turkoman rugs often look brighter and better after thirty or forty years of use.

A Tapestry of Music and Dance

Afghan folk music probably differed from one tribal group to another in the past. Over the centuries, however, it has blended quite a bit. The radio has done much to cause this blending. There is no record industry, and most people rarely see a professional band. What they mostly hear, therefore, is the radio. The only station in the country is Radio Kabul. You might say that Afghan popular music is "the Radio Kabul style."

This music mixes the sound of Indian film music and of many Afghan folk styles. The songs are melodic. Admired male singers have rich, mellow voices. Female singers often have high, reedy ones. A traditional band will have three or four players. One will play *tabla*, which are two little congalike drums. Another will play the *armunia* (harmonium), a small hand-pumped organ. A third may play a stringed instrument such as the short heavy *rebab*, which has seventeen strings or more. You might hear a band like this at a traditional village wedding.

Not all bands, however, are traditional. Many Afghan

Two musicians. One is playing tabla *and the other is playing a* rebab.

pop singers of today were influenced by a man named Ahmad Zahir. He began his career in the midsixties and was murdered in the late seventies. Ahmad Zahir is sometimes called the Elvis Presley of Afghanistan. Today, in Kabul, many pop stars play the accordion, Ahmad Zahir's favorite instrument. A band at a Kabul wedding may play electric guitars, electric keyboards, and Western-style rock-and-roll drums.

Weddings and dancing go together. Afghans do not, however, dance with partners. At a wedding or other party, one person at a time will get up to dance, while others simply watch and cheer. The dancer makes many snakelike movements of the arms, hands, and fingers. When one dancer sits down, another jumps up to perform. Men and women usually party in separate rooms, if not in separate houses. At the men's party, therefore, the spectators and dancers are all men. At the women's party, they are all women. In Kabul, however, men and women may all celebrate a wedding in the same room.

At a public festival you might see the Pushtoon folk dance, the *attan*. A circle of dancers are needed for this dance. Those who are not dancing beat big drums called *dohls*, or honk away on *surnais*—horns that sound like bagpipes. Any number of people can join the circle. Sometimes hundreds of dancers dance outdoors for hours.

The war has tossed the Afghan way of life into the air like a deck of cards. How the cards will land when the war fades, no one knows. Life will be different, of course, and everybody knows it. Afghans only hope it will have some of the easygoing, life-loving qualities of the past.

3. Crossroads of Conquest

One word sums up the history of the land that is now called Afghanistan: conflict. Throughout the centuries, people have come pushing from north, west, and south, only to clash in the Hindu Kush. The players have changed many times, but the game remains the same. No one people has been able to claim this land totally and shut out all others. That constant struggle—not a core people or culture—has set Afghanistan apart as a separate country.

Early records of the Persian Empire do speak of "afghan" tribes living in the Hindu Kush mountains, but the word was used as a description. It meant "howlers," "troublemakers," or "warriors," depending on who you ask. Were those "afghan" tribes the ancestors of the true Afghan tribes of today—the Pushtoons? No one knows.

One thing is certain. The name, culture, and borders of this land have shifted many times. In the fourth century B.C., for example, it was an eastern province of the Persian Empire. Most of the people worshiped fire and followed the religion of a prophet called Zoroaster. Then in 331 B.C., Alexander the Great and his Greek armies toppled the Persian Empire.

The Greeks then came rampaging through Afghan-

istan and so, for two hundred years, Afghanistan was
divided up among various Greek kingdoms.

The Greeks were driven out by mysterious Caucasian
nomads called Kushans, who set up a rich kingdom that
lasted four hundred years. In their time, Afghanistan
became a Buddhist region. When Kushan power faded,
the Indians came pushing up from the south. They in turn
were driven out by Huns from the north. By the sixth
century A.D., however, the Ephthalite kingdom of the
Huns had crumbled, too. The Persians were back in
control of western Afghanistan. Hindu kings had risen to
power in and around Kabul. Most of the people were still
Buddhist. And then something happened that would
change Afghanistan forever.

Revelation in a Distant Cave

The event in question took place far away, near the
Arabian city of Mecca. A camel driver named Muhammad
was fasting in a cave one day. Suddenly the angel Gabriel
appeared and commanded him to write. Muhammad
wrote a verse of the Koran. The religion of Islam was
born. Soon all of Arabia had converted to Islam. By the
time the Prophet died, Arabia had become an expanding
Muslim state.

Fifty years later, Arab armies were knocking at the
gates of Kabul. The fighting in Afghanistan lasted nearly

The Kushans carved this fifty-three-meter-high Buddha—the world's largest standing Buddha—into a cliff in central Afghanistan.

a hundred years. One legend tells of the "Two-Sworded King" who helped to conquer Kabul.

He fought, supposedly, with a sword in each hand. His head was cut off in the battle but he simply tucked it under his arm and kept on swinging. Arabs conquered Afghanistan and then quickly lost control of it. Islam, however, scored a lasting triumph. By A.D. 750 only small pockets of non-Muslims remained in and around the Hindu Kush.

The first thousand years of the Muslim era in Afghanistan belong to the Turks and Mongols of the northern steppes. A peak moment came in the tenth century with the Turkish emperor Sultan Mahmud the Ghaznivid. From his capital in Ghazni (near Kabul), Mahmud ruled an empire that stretched from the heart of India deep into modern-day Iran. Mahmud was a military genius—but he also loved beauty, literature, and learning. He filled Ghazni with gorgeous mosques and public buildings. He supported more than nine hundred scholars, philosophers, and poets at his court. Most of them wrote in Dari, even though their emperor was Turkish: Dari was considered the language of culture throughout central Asia in those days.

Perhaps the lowest moment in Afghan history came in the twelfth century. Genghis Khan, a ferocious Mongol warrior from the northeast, attacked the Muslim world. Genghis and his Mongol horsemen massacred entire cities. They wrecked canals. They plowed salt into the finest farmlands. They dumped the great library of Balkh into the Oxus River. The library had a million volumes, according to legend, enough to choke the river. But the current soon washed the books away. Balkh was once called "the Mother of Cities." Now it is a dusty little town, surrounded by ruins and rubble. Timur-i-lang ("Timur the Lame One") was the next brutal conquerer. A descendant of Genghis Khan, he burst from the northern steppes in the fourteenth century. About two hundred years later came Timur's descendant, Babur. From his

The ruins of Shar-i-Gholghola, a city in central Afghanistan, which was destroyed by Genghis Khan in the twelfth century. The entire population of the city was massacred.

capital in Kabul, this colorful poet-adventurer conquered India and founded the Moghul dynasty. One of Babur's descendants built the Taj Mahal. Babur's tomb in Kabul has long been a beloved public garden.

Birth of a Nation

Throughout these early centuries, the Hindu Kush region was never called Afghanistan. It was called by such names as *Ariana*, *Bactria*, and *Khorasan*. But now at last a people known as Afghans rose to power in the region.

These Afghans, or Pushtoons as they were also called, lived in the mountains. In the mid-1700s, a young man named Ahmad Shah united the Pushtoon tribes. He then did what so many Turkish chiefs had done before. He swooped down from the Hindu Kush, sacked Indian cities, hauled back treasure, and knocked together a sprawling empire. People called his empire Afghanistan—"land of the Afghans."

But Afghan/Pushtoon power flared just as Europeans were entering the scene. Great Britain was colonizing India just then. The Russians were pressing down from the north. Squeezed between these forces, Ahmad Shah's empire shrank like a drying sponge.

The Russians wanted Afghanistan for strategic reasons. They hoped to capture a warm-water port on the Indian Ocean. From the southern slopes of the Hindu Kush, they felt they could launch a successful attack (as so many others had done). The British, however, prized India for its enormous wealth. They didn't want the Russians to get an inch of their precious colony. To hold the Russians back, the British decided to conquer Afghanistan themselves.

The British and Afghans fought three wars. The first one ended with the massacre of all the British forces on the road between Kabul and Peshawar. Only one British citizen escaped the country alive in that winter of 1842.

A few years later the British tried again. The most

famous battle of the second war took place at Maiwand in 1880. The Afghan heroine Malalai rallied the Afghans by waving her veil as a flag and shouting stirring war poetry. The Afghans won the battle, only to discover they had already lost the war. The Afghan and British governments had just signed the Treaty of Gundumuk. This treaty drew the borders of the country where they run to this day. It allowed Afghan kings to run the country any way they pleased but put the British in charge of Afghanistan's foreign policy—its dealing with other countries. For the British, this was good enough. The treaty made Afghanistan a buffer state, a barrier between the Russians and the Indian subcontinent.

After the war, a new king named Amir Abdu'Rahman came to power. As a young boy, according to one story, Abdu'Rahman killed a rabid camel with a single blow from a stone. He was a fearsome man. In earlier times, such a king would have built an empire. But the Russians and British kept him fenced in. So Abdur'Rahman set out to conquer his own country. He fought seventeen campaigns inside Afghanistan and brought all the tribes and lords and little kingdoms under his control. He was the first to forge Afghanistan into what we think of as a country: a land with definite borders, ruled by one central power. Abdu'Rahman's grandson, King Amanullah, launched the third Afghan–British war in 1919. In one month of war and two years of peace talks, the Afghans gained total independence from the British. Thus, in 1921, the modern state of Afghanistan was born.

Reign of a Royal Gentleman

The last king of Afghanistan took the throne in 1933. His name was Zahir Shah and he reigned for forty years. Zahir Shah was a pleasant gentleman who liked to hunt and hike. For thirty years he left the ruling mostly to his relatives. First his uncles ran the country. Then one of his cousins took over. Members of the king's clan, the Mohammadzais, held most of the top government jobs, but this was nothing new: The Mohammadzais had ruled Afghanistan since 1826.

Under Zahir and his relatives, Afghanistan inched into the modern age. The Kabul government built schools and highways. After the Second World War (which passed almost unnoticed here), money started pouring in from both the Soviet Union and the United States, who were competing for allies around the globe. The Kabul government used this money to set up factories, dam rivers, and build canals. Meanwhile, the Mohammadzais tried cautiously to bring Afghan women into public life. Girls began going to school, and some women began working at government jobs. In 1959 Prime Minister Daoud, the king's cousin, did away with the law that women had to wear chadris.

But while Kabul changed rapidly, the rest of the country did not keep pace. The government projects made many people of the countryside uneasy. They suspected that the government was trying to interfere with their way of life. These suspicions planted the seeds of the future war.

In 1964, King Zahir made a bold move. He set up an elected parliament and had a new constitution written. He fired all his relatives from high office, including his cousin Daoud. This was a risky move. As prime minister, Daoud had been the real ruler of Afghanistan.

Under the New Democracy, the king allowed Afghans to form political parties and publish their own newspapers. At once, all sorts of political parties sprang up. One of them was a Communist party called the People's Democratic Party of Afghanistan (PDPA). It was not the only Communist party. It was the only one, however, that believed in Soviet-style Communism.

Although the PDPA had only about thirty members, it quickly split into two factions called *Khalq* ("The People") and Parcham ("The Banner"). Both Khalq and Parcham began to gain followers in the army. Daoud, the fallen prime minister, watched with interest. Finally, he made a deal with the Communists to help him overthrow the king. The plot worked and King Zahir was exiled to Italy. Daoud took over as president. Then he began plotting to get rid of his Communist allies.

But the Communists were hatching plots, too. One day in 1978, Daoud heard the Communists were planning to attack his palace on April 27. When the day came, he stationed a ring of tanks around his palace. He had no idea that the commander of his tanks was secretly a member of Khalq. At noon, the tanks all turned and pointed their guns inward. Daoud and his three thousand personal bodyguards put up a fierce fight, but the odds were hopeless. He, his family, and all his guards were killed. By nightfall, Khalq and Parcham had seized control of the government.

Reforms at Gunpoint

Khalq and Parcham divided the government jobs between themselves. Then they moved against all their possible rivals. They arrested Mohammadzais. They attacked members of other political parties, driving their leaders into the hills. They jailed people who had been educated in Western countries. Then they invited several thousand Soviet advisors to come in and help them manage the country. The new regime set out to make extreme changes in Afghanistan by force. They took land away from big landowners called *khans* and split it up among poor, landless farmers. But they did not work out a way to get water and seed to the farmers. When the crops failed, the farmers turned against the new government.

The Communists believed in education for women.
They sent soldiers and teachers to villages and ordered
that women attend these schools. The village men didn't
want strangers from the city to even see their women.
The men refused to let the women of their households go
to the new schools. Soldiers then broke into their homes
and tried to take the women away by force. Clashes broke
out, and people were killed. Soon people began rebelling
against the new government. In March 1979, a huge
uprising broke out in the city of Herat. The government
bombed the city, killing hundreds of ordinary people.
Afterwards, thousands more Soviet advisors poured into
Aghanistan to help the Afghan army fight the growing
rebellion.

Meanwhile, Chairman Taraki, leader of the country,
tried to shoot his own deputy, Hafizullah Amin. He
missed and ended up under arrest himself. Three weeks
later Taraki was dead and Amin was president. Amin
stepped up the war and clamped down much harder on
protest. He put thousands of people in jail for such crimes
as listening to foreign radio stations. Yet the rebellion
only grew and spread. By December 1979, the Communist
government seemed to be teetering.

A Crushing Force from the North

That year, just before New Year's, the Soviet Union

invaded Afghanistan with 110,000 troops. They killed Amin and replaced him with Babrak Karmal, the leader of Parcham. Then the Soviets launched a war to crush the rebellion in the countryside. This invasion shocked the world. The United Nations condemned it and called for the Soviet Union to withdraw. President Carter of the United States banned the sale of American grain to punish the Soviets. He pulled America out of the 1980 Moscow Olympics.

For forty years, the United States and the Soviet Union had been locked in a "Cold War." This so-called war was really a deadly competition for allies. Neither country had dared attack the other because both had nuclear weapons. Instead, they had supported opposite sides in small wars around the world.

By invading Afghanistan, the Soviet Union seemed willing to risk a "hot" war with America. Why? Some experts said the Soviet Union simply could not bear to let a Communist government fall. Others said the Soviets were reviving the old Russian plan: to hack a path to a warm-water port on the Indian Ocean. Still others claimed the invasion marked a warlike turn in Soviet policy as a whole. They said the Soviets would now try to take over the whole globe by military force.

But the invasion of Afghanistan marked a very different kind of turn for the Soviet Union. As the war dragged on, the Soviet military lost its air of invincible

*The Kandahar region commander Mullah Naquib and his stinger.
Stingers helped Afghanistan win the war against the Soviet Union.*

might. Soviet prestige faded around the globe. Soviet soldiers came home in coffins and something unusual began to happen. Soviet citizens began to complain out loud.

To make matters worse, the war went badly. From the United States, the rebels acquired shoulder-fired missile launchers called stingers. With these cheap devices, one man could shoot down an expensive warplane. The Soviets had to pour millions of dollars into the war every day. Yet, after nine years of war, they had made no gains. So at last, in 1989, the Soviets decided to give up on victory and just get out. The Soviet withdrawal from Afghanistan was part of a worldwide change: Communism, it seemed, was running out of steam and the Cold War was ending. Some said the withdrawal from Afghanistan helped end the Cold War. Others said the end of the Cold War brought about the withdrawal. Either way, one thing is clear: The Afghans handed the Soviet Union its first real setback since World War II.

The Struggle Goes On

The Soviets are gone now, but Soviet money and guns are still flowing into Kabul. The rebels continue to get weapons, too. The fighting continues.

Most of the people of Kabul consider themselves Muslims. Few feel loyal to Najibullah, the current president. And yet the people of Kabul do not want to be ruled by the Mujahideen, the Islamic rebels of the countryside. The government in Kabul, meanwhile, claims it is no longer Communist. It has changed its name to Hizbi Watan—the National Party. But Afghans outside the cities do not believe it has really changed. They still do not accept its rule.

The countryside is ruled by hundreds of "commanders" and each is like a little king. Few are willing to obey any central government, nor will they bow to one another. The quarrel between the commanders is not over ideas or policies. It is over power. Most of the commanders in the south are Pushtoons, who have dominated Afghanistan for two hundred years. Other tribes are not eager to submit to Pushtoons again if they have a choice. Perhaps the most powerful commander on the scene today is Ahmad Shah Masoud, a Tajik. The Uzbeks, however, have their Hafizullah Arbab. The Farsiwans have Ismail Khan. And there are many others. Perhaps one of these men will weld the broken pieces of Afghanistan into a new nation. In the meantime, the old drumbeat of this land goes on: struggle.

4. A Society of Storytellers

As a child my favorite author was K'koh. No one outside my family ever heard of her, however. K'koh never published her works, because she couldn't write. All her skill went into telling her tales out loud.

Virtually no one in Afghanistan has access to books, movies, television, or video games. Storytelling remains, therefore, a major form of entertainment. Most adult Afghans are skillful storytellers and every family has its own stars. K'koh—my grandmother—was one of ours.

K'koh specialized in a type of story usually told to the very young. These stories feature a great deal of rhyming, repetition, and humorous nonsense. They are somewhat like nursery rhymes, only longer—and they have a plot. Some parts are chanted in a sing-song voice, but other parts are spoken like any story. "The Three Sons of Mah'madyar" is a good example. Like all Afghan folktales it begins with the line *Bood Nabood*—"There was/there wasn't . . ." In this case, Bood Nabood the three sons of Mah'madyar—

"At mealtime, always able and quick,
At worktime, always pale and sick."

In every version of the tale, one of the boys goes on a journey. He keeps running across items that seem count-

This man, like most adult Afghans, is a skillful storyteller.

less at first sight but add up to only three on second glance. Two of the items are always no good and the third is even worse. The son of Mah'madyar always chooses item number three.

When he goes hunting, for example, he has a choice of so many guns, so many guns, that all in all they add up to three guns. Two of these guns don't shoot so well; the third one has no stock and lacks a barrel. The boy picks the third gun and off he goes a-hunting. After many adventures, he ends up in a house without a roof, boiling a bird with no flesh, in a pot with no bottom, over a fire with no heat, in water ladled from a bone-dry ditch, to make a soup you can just imagine. And the story ends, as they all do, with a little saying: "God gave him what he deserved, may God give us what we deserve, too."

Two Kinds of Fools

Traditional tales for older Afghan children often center around stock characters such as Bachey Kul, or "the Bald Boy." Bachey Kul is not really one particular character but a type—or rather two types. Sometimes he is a cunning rascal. Sometimes he is an utter numbskull. Either way, he always wins.

The cunning Bald Boy is often the youngest of many sons. His older brothers have cut him out of his inheritance, so he sets off to seek his own fortune. His wanderings take him through a string of adventures that can last as long as the night. Through trickery, the Bald Boy beats each of the ghouls (or demons), giants, robbers, and other enemies he meets. Eventually, he wins a princess and a kingdom and gets the last laugh on his brothers.

On the other hand, the Bald Boy may be an utter fool. In one such story, the Bald Boy's mother gets him a job. The first day he gets a pound of butter as payment. He carries it home in his hands, and it melts. "Wrap your payment in a damp cloth next time," his mother advises him, "Carry it under your shirt." The Bald Boy follows her advice but with bad results, for the next day his payment is a puppy. And so it goes: The Bald Boy always follows yesterday's advice. It never fits today's payment. Finally he ends up carrying a donkey home on his back. The sight makes a princess burst out laughing. This princess happens to be choking on a bone. Laughing makes the bone come out and saves her life. The king rewards the Bald Boy by letting him marry the princess and making him a prince.

Quite a different sort of fool is the beloved Mullah Nasruddin. A mullah is a Muslim religious teacher and leader. Mullahs are respected figures and many of them have a great deal of power, but people do poke friendly fun at them: They are not sacred like the Koran, the Prophet, or the religion itself. Stories about Mullah

Nasruddin are told throughout the Muslim world. In Afghanistan, everybody seems to know hundreds. If one person in a group tells a Mullah Nasruddin story, someone else is sure to remember two more. These stories, therefore, tend to come in bunches. The Mullah is always a fool, but sometimes he is a wise fool. For example:

The Mullah borrowed a huge pot from his neighbor one time and kept it for a week. When he finally returned it, the neighbor found a little pot inside.

"What's this?" the neighbor asked.

"Your pot got pregnant at my house," said the Mullah. "Last night it gave birth to this baby pot."

"Very well," said the neighbor, quite happy to get a new pot for free.

The next time Mullah asked to borrow the big pot, his neighbor lent it very willingly. But this time two weeks passed and the Mullah still had not returned the pot. The neighbor came calling. "Where is my pot?" he demanded.

"Your pot died," said Mullah.

"But how can a pot possibly die?" the man ranted.

"A pot that can have a baby can certainly die," the Mullah said and shrugged.

Sometimes, however, as in this story, the Mullah is just silly.

Mullah Nasruddin was standing in a long line at the baker's shop one day. He got tired of waiting so he played a little trick. "I hear the baker on the other side of town is

selling bread at half price today," he murmured. The
rumor spread up the line and soon all the other customers
drifted off. Now it was the Mullah's turn to order bread.
But wait, he thought. Why should I be the only one to buy
bread at full price? And off he hurried to the other bakery
where he found himself once again at the end of the line.

Doomed Lovers and Mighty Heroes

Central Asian poets have long shaped great literature out
of stories borrowed from folklore. Folklore, meanwhile,
keeps borrowing the stories back. An expert Afghan
storyteller may fill a whole dark winter evening with a
long story of love or heroism, borrowed from Dari/Farsi
literature and changed in any way the storyteller pleases.

Among Dari-speaking Afghans, the most popular
love story is the one about Leilah and Majnun. Two great
poets, Nizami and Jami, wrote versions of this tale. In
Nizami's version, Leilah and Majnun grew up together
and fell in love. But Leilah's father would not let them
marry because Majnun was poor. He forced Leilah to
marry a powerful man she did not love. Maddened by
grief, Majnun wandered away into the desert. He made
friends with the beasts and learned their language. Years
later, he returned home to find that Leilah's husband had
died. At last he and Leilah could get together. But when
the lovers met and talked, they found they had nothing in

common. Majnun just seemed crazy to Leilah. She seemed cold and unfeeling to him. So Majnun went howling back to the desert, where he died of a broken heart among the animals. After he left, Leilah pined away, too, because life had lost all meaning for her.

Stories of doomed lovers are popular throughout Afghanistan and every group has its own favorites. The Pushtoons, for example, tell the story of Khadi and Marghalai, cousins who fell in love. Khadi was too poor to marry Marghalai, so he went off to seek his fortune. Years later, he came back, a rich man disguised as a peddler. He found that Marghalai was the happily married wife of another man and mother of many children. Khadi's father meanwhile had died of grief at the loss of his son. Brokenhearted, Khadi moved on.

Other long stories present swashbuckling adventures. Many feature characters from the *Shahnama, the Book of Kings*. The *Shahnama* was written in Afghanistan, for a Turkish emperor, about the rise of the Iranian people. It features villains like Zahak, a brain-eating monster with snakes growing from his shoulders. The greatest of its many heroes is Rustum—the "elephant-bodied" and "lionhearted." His mighty horse, Rakhsh, can see the footprints of an ant at two leagues. Rustum is always going on quests, battling lions bare-handed, killing giants, and saving his king from wizards and demons.

Stories about heroes also come from real-life figures.

Most groups have folktales about their own mighty warriors. One tribe's hero may be another tribe's villain. In a valley called Kohistan, the people tell stories about the great warrior Habibullah Ghazi. This Habibullah was a Tajik bandit who overthrew the Pushtoon government in 1929 and ruled Afghanistan for nine months. Among the Pushtoons, the same man is remembered as Bachey Saqao— "the Water Carrier's Boy." Their stories paint him as a brutal, ignorant buffoon.

The Invisible Ones

One strange creature found in Afghan folklore is the *Jinn.* Jinn stories are meant to make you shiver, just like ghost stories here in America. But Jinn stories are different from ghost stories in one important way. Afghans really believe in Jinns. After all, the Koran mentions this strange race. Jinns, according to the Koran, are made of smokeless fire. They can be visible or invisible. They can change their shape at will. Afghans often tell of sighting them in lonely places such as ancient ruins and old deserted mills. In one typical story, a man claimed he saw an enormous fellow lying in a graveyard one night. The fellow measured twenty or thirty feet from head to foot. Tiny people no more than a hand high swarmed all over him. Anecdotes like this are common. Unexplained lights, strange noises, things that go bump in the night—all can provide the seed for a Jinn anecdote. Probably the stories tend to grow in the retelling.

Afghans believe that Jinns can enter other living beings. Jinns often appear as cats, they say—especially as gray ones. This is not to say that all cats are Jinns, but any cat might be one. The mere possibility gives Afghans squeamish feelings about cats.

Superstitious Afghans also believe that Jinns can enter or get trapped inside of human beings. And indeed, occasionally, some Afghans do go into a wild state, in which they howl, babble, and fling themselves about. Bystanders clear breakables out of the way and wait anxiously for the Jinn to get flung out. Sometimes they may call in the mullah or some special healer to chase the Jinn away with words from the Koran. Folk healers sell amulets for people to wear around their necks. These amulets supposedly keep out Jinns and ward off evil.

Thrilling heroes and doomed lovers serve to make a long night short. The lovable mullah and the clever Bald Boy raise a smile. But sometimes, as darkness falls, you sense another presence in the room if you're an Afghan. That's when you remember the invisible ones who share your world and you wonder: Has a Jinn wandered in to hear the story, too? When you're young, that thought's enough to make you huddle closer to the storyteller.

5. Festive Days

In the Afghan calendar, the year begins on March 21. Nature provides a great sense of renewal at this time, especially for a society of farmers and herders. Trees are putting out new buds; animals are having babies. No wonder, then, that *Nowroz*, or New Year's Day, is one of the brightest and busiest of Afghan holidays.

After months of hiding from the bitter Afghan winter, people gladly spill outdoors to celebrate Nowroz at great open-air fairs. In the cities, the fair can spread through an entire neighborhood. In the country, a village fair can draw folks from miles around. Often, a carnival sets up at the fair. It offers hand-operated wooden Ferris wheels, merry-go-rounds, and other rides. Children can buy wooden New Year's toys, such as the ever popular *ghirghiras*, an L-shaped device that makes a clacking sound when swung around. Adults can try their hand at games of chance, or watch or take part in competitions such as tree-planting contests. Street vendors sell boiled eggs, fried fish, and the *jelabis* that are eaten with fish. Jelabis are bright yellow fried pretzels, dripping with honey. Some people like to dye their animals on New Year's Day. Children delight in the sight of green chickens or purple sheep.

Not everybody goes to the fair at Nowroz. Some children join their elders in a round of traditional New Year's visiting, quick casual visits to a series of households. At each stop the visitors drink some tea and accept a bowl of *Haft Miwa*, or "Seven Fruits." Haft Miwa is a cold soup of fruit and nuts made and served only at Nowroz. A second name for it is therefore "New Year's Fruit." You might like to try this recipe for Haft Miwa. Start your soup four or five days ahead of time.

Haft Miwa

1 cup skinned almonds (unsalted)
1 cup skinned walnuts (unsalted)
1 cup skinned pistachios (unsalted)
1 cup dried peaches
1 cup red raisins
1 cup green raisins
1 cup dried apricots
6 cups water

If using salted nuts, rinse off any salt. ☛Put the nuts in one bowl and the dried fruits in another. ☛Pour 3 cups of cold water into each bowl. ☛Stir, cover, and put both bowls into the refrigerator. ☛After two days, combine the ingredients into one large bowl. ☛Stir, cover, and let the soup steep for two or three more days in the refrigerator. Then, it is ready to eat.

Reverent Rejoicing

The two main religious holidays of the year are both called Eid. *Eid-i-Qurban*, a four-day holiday, celebrates an event from religious history: God asked the prophet Ibrahim (Abraham) to sacrifice his son and Ibrahim set out to obey. Suddenly the angel Gabriel appeared and had Ibrahim sacrifice a sheep instead of his son. The story dramatizes the central belief of Islam: the need for absolute obedience to God's will.

Eid-i-Qurban (called Eid-ul-Azhar in Arabic) comes at the end of the month of *Hajj*, when Muslim pilgrims go to Mecca. The pilgrims sacrifice a sheep as part of their ceremonies. Those who stay home also slaughter a sheep if they can afford it. They roast it whole if possible and feed the poor. People go to the mosque for communal prayers during this holiday and get together with their families for feasting and celebration. Friends sometimes exchange gifts.

Eid-i-Qurban is a rather solemn holiday. Not so the other great religious holiday, *Eid-i-Ramazan* (Eid-ul-Fitr in Arabic). This Eid celebrates the end of Ramazan, the month of fasting. During Ramazan a great sense of sharing builds up, because everybody is going through the same hardship. The whole month thus lays the ground-work for the joy of Eid.

Each morning during Ramazan, those who plan to

fast get up before dawn and have a light snack. Children are not required to fast, but many children try to, anyway. They set small goals for themselves: to fast one whole day, for example, or to fast until noon every day for a week. Just getting up with the grown-ups in the early morning darkness can be a special feeling for children.

Every evening, people gather outdoors at dusk, waiting for that moment when "the eye can no longer tell a white thread from a black one." When the moment comes, a signal sounds. In a village a voice starts chanting from the mosque. In Kabul, a cannon fires. Whatever the signal, everybody breaks their fast at that same moment. Later they enjoy a complete meal. But the next morning, the hardship begins again.

Keeping to the fast grows even harder as the month wears on. Therefore, when the Eid dawns at last, the sense of celebration spreads like brushfire. No funerals may be held during Ramazan: Islam forbids mourning on these three days. Everybody gets new clothes for Eid. If the adults cannot afford it, at least they get new clothes for the children. Even in modern war-torn Afghanistan, battle-field commanders try their best to get new Eid clothes for their fighting men.

Most of all, people rejoice with their families at Eid by getting together for communal feasts. If an extended family lives in several households they may gather at a different household each day. Households that do not get

These women and children wear new clothes for Eid.

their turn complain bitterly and squabble for rights to the first feast on the next Eid.

Muslims calculate all religious events on the lunar calendar and the lunar year is eleven days shorter than the solar one. Each year, therefore, the Eid festivals start eleven days earlier. This means that the Eid festivals travel through all the different seasons. They make a full cycle in the course of thirty three years.

Wedding Merriment: Dancing for Days

Weddings surely rank as the biggest celebrations in Afghanistan. A good village wedding can last for days. But the party only caps a tide of celebration that has probably been rising for months. To begin with, a young man in Afghanistan does not do his own courting or proposing. A group of women from his family do this work by "going *talab-gari*." That is, they make a series of visits to the girl's family. With each visit they drop hints and more hints of their intentions. Finally they make the proposal of marriage. If the girl's people accept, they serve a special cone of sugar to the boy's family on the next visit. In modern Kabul, a boy and girl may go on dates and even arrange their own marriage. Even so, for the sake of tradition, their families may go through a slight ritual of talab-gari.

After the proposal and acceptance comes the *shirni-khuri* or "candy-eating" party. At this party the groom's family gives little gifts to the bride. The shirni-khuri marks the formal engagement and it can be a rousing party in its own right.

Nothing compares to the main event, however, the wedding itself. For a real village wedding, guests gather for days and the celebration can go on for a week or more. The ceremony itself stretches over three nights. Separate men's and women's parties take place at the groom's and bride's houses every night. Hired musicians play at each location and children flow back and forth between the houses, reporting to each party what the other group is doing.

The high point of the wedding comes on the third night when the bride finally makes her way to the groom's house. In the main party room, two chairs decorated like thrones sit upon a platform. The groom is already sitting in his chair and the bride advances slowly toward hers. The band plays *Austa Biro,* or *"Go Slowly,"* the wedding song. The guests clap and cheer and sing along. Everybody who remembers the title remembers the words, for they are simply:

"Go slowly. Go slowly. Oh, bride, go slowly."

The bride does her best to oblige. She inches along at the slowest pace she can manage without actually stopping. A young female relative walks along behind her with a pot of the reddish brown paste called henna buried in a heap of flowers. After many rituals and vows, the bride and groom both get a dab of the henna tied to their hands with a cloth. The henna stains the skin red and the honeymoon is supposed to last as long as the stain is there. No sooner does the wedding couple finish with the henna than children swarm over the tray, clamoring for henna of their own. Most or all of the children at a wedding party end up with red palms.

The ceremony ends with the guests flinging candy-coated almonds at the wedding couple. Boys scatter to gather them as they fall. Those who collect almonds from the groom's clothes supposedly improve their own chances of a good marriage. Of course, the custom differs a little from one ethnic group to another. Among the Turkoman tribes, for example, at a certain point, the groom and his relatives pretend to capture the bride from her father's house. The bride's relatives make a show of driving them off by pelting them with eggs.

Weddings and other big celebrations are fun for children because they get to be with so many other children. Close relatives arrive one or two days early to help with the cooking, and with them come the cousins.

Adults rarely organize activities for children. They leave the kids to themselves, except when snagging them for chores, and the kids make up their own games.

Often, some or all of the guests sleep over. And since Afghans drink lots of tea and no alcohol, they tend to stay up late at parties. No one sends the children to bed at some certain hour. They can stay up, sharing in the games and fun, as long as they can keep their eyes open. When they run out of energy, they simply find a blanket, crawl into a suitable corner, and go to sleep, with the hubbub of the party still boiling around them.

6. Within the Compound Walls

Almost every nonnomadic family in Afghanistan lives in some sort of compound—that is, a yard with a wall around it. The compound wall divides two whole worlds. It keeps the private life of the family and clan separate from the public world of trade, politics, work, and war. Walking through an Afghan city or village, therefore, what you mainly see surrounding you are walls.

Today, many of these walls are broken and compounds stand empty because of the war. Women, children, and old people have moved to Pakistan, where they live as refugees. The men and even the teenage boys move back and forth from the camps to the battlefields within the country, where they live in tents or bunkers. Yet wherever possible, as much as possible, Afghans keep trying to patch together the kind of family life they have lived and cherished for centuries.

Imagine yourself as an Afghan child living within Afghanistan in a village that is still inhabited. What might you see when you come home from the fields and open the gates of your compound?

If you live in a traditional compound, you will probably enter through a tunnel that runs under part of the house and brings you into an open courtyard. All the

Streets in an Afghan village. Here, everyone lives in a compound. Walking down the street, a person sees only walls.

rooms are built around the edges. In the yard you will find a well and a garden. If you live in a village, you also find a stable for the animals—a sheep or two, and perhaps a cow.

The family dog may be lounging in the yard as well. It will never be allowed into the house, for Afghans consider dogs unclean (the only pets Afghans allow into the house are birds).

View of a compound interior.

A Tour of the Compound

From the gate, you can get to a guest room without passing all the way through the courtyard. This allows the family to entertain outsiders without letting them see the private life of the household. The guest room may be the best-furnished room in the house, but if you live in a village or an old-fashioned city household, it contains no chairs or tables. Afghans prefer to sit on the floor. The guest room, therefore, has cotton-stuffed mats and pillows along the edges of the room. Visitors take off their shoes near the door, sit on one of the mattresses, and lean back against the wall, cushioned by a pillow. When tea is served, individual teapots, tea bowls, and dishes of nuts, raisins, and candy are set on the floor in front of each guest.

Other rooms probably open onto the courtyard. They include a kitchen and an outhouse. Except in large cities, the kitchen is equipped with nothing but a sort of barbecue pit. Few village households have electricity or gas, so women cook over wood or charcoal fires. To bake rice, for example, they put the pot on a bed of coals and pile more chunks of red-hot charcoal on the lid. Since they have no refrigerators, they use only fresh or dried ingredients in cooking. Since they have no running water, they dip water out of a bucket filled at the family well. In Kabul, by contrast, most households have running water, electricity, and other conveniences.

In small villages and country forts, each compound has its own bread-baking oven. Bread is the most important item of any Afghan's diet. In fact, *naan*, the word for "bread," is commonly used to mean "food." Afghan bread is made from whole wheat and shaped like a flat football about fifteen or twenty inches from end to end. In a household that bakes its own bread, the women have to get up very early to start the fire. As you can see, daily life in an Afghan village is hard work.

Any other rooms look pretty much like the guest

room—by day. They have cotton mats along the edges and a rug in the middle. Old-fashioned Afghan households do not have special rooms set aside for use as bedrooms or dining rooms. Wherever the family happens to be at mealtime, a cloth is spread on the floor. This turns the sitting room into a dining room. At bedtime, blankets or quilts come out of closets or trunks. The dining room becomes a bedroom. In the morning, the bedding goes back into storage. Bedrooms become sitting rooms again.

A Divided World

The compound walls reflect a crucial fact. If you're an Afghan, you live in a divided world. On one side of the line is the clan, all the people you're related to. On the other side are *beganas*—"strangers"—all the people you're not related to. Life in the private world of the clan is warm, cozy, dramatic, rich, and intense. Life among the strangers may be interesting and you may have good friends out there. Still, the fact remains, those people are all "strangers."

The divided world makes life very different for men and women, especially because this is a Muslim country. Islam teaches that women belong in the private world of the home and family. Men have a duty to protect and shelter this private world. Furthermore, Islam frowns on flirting, dating, or any kind of romantic friendship be-

A pot boils on the fire in the kitchen.

tween unmarried men and women. It has rules to keep unrelated men and women from mixing socially. This is why, in many Afghan households, outsiders are not supposed to even see the women of a household.

Within the clan, men and women live in the same world. They have very different roles, but women have a strong voice. Outside the clan, women have almost no role. The public world is a male world.

At least, such is the case in the countryside, where Islamic ways hold sway. The Mujahideen, who are fighting the Communist government, want to strengthen this divided way of life. The refugees in Pakistan would like to live a strongly divided life, but find it difficult to do so in the camps. Afghan women in these camps complain bitterly about their lack of privacy.

In Kabul, even before the Communists took power, the outer face of life had changed. Women went to public places. Many worked outside the home, at government jobs or in private offices. A few earned degrees in medicine and other professions. Women were elected to the parliament, when there was one. Boys and girls even went on dates. Deep down, however, even in Kabul, people remain closest to their family and clan. Even here, most Afghans still live within a walled compound. They still think of the clan and the family as an inner world. They may enjoy mixing with members of other families, but outsiders remain outsiders.

There is little privacy in the refugee camps in Pakistan. This is especially hard on Afghan women living in the camps.

The Village of Relatives

Almost everything that counts for an Afghan takes place within the compound walls—within the family. The family, however, is a large group. It may include a hundred people or more. It may be divided into any number of households living in different compounds. In a village, these compounds may be clustered in the same place, but in a city, they may be strung out through various neighborhoods. Either way, an Afghan's home is not just the compound in which he or she lives. It is all the compounds of his or her extended family. In Kabul, such a network of compounds makes a sort of village within the city. Really, then, every Afghan lives in a village. And all the other people in the village are his or her relatives.

This "village of relatives" provides most of the close relationships an Afghan enjoys. It is here that an Afghan finds friendship, love, and work. It is here that he or she finds romance as well—for most Afghans marry one of their relatives. Clan gossip takes the place of soap opera: old grudges, buried secrets, budding friendships, heartless stepmothers, feuds, and marriages—there is never a shortage of drama in an Afghan village.

When you step into your compound, you step into your own village. It is such a different world that even your name changes. On the outside you may be called Najiba or Leila or Mahmoud or Omar. Inside the family compound, however, after a certain age, you acquire a family nickname, or *laqub*. These nicknames consist of the same few words put together in different ways. Words found in nicknames, for example, include "candy," "sweet," "flower," "lion," "chief," "uncle," "daddy," "lady," and "dear." Typical nicknames, therefore, might be "Lion Uncle," "Flower Dear," "Sweet Lady," "Flower Daddy," and "Uncle Candy."

The few stock words found in family nicknames can probably be combined in just enough ways to cover all the members of one large extended family. That is quite enough, because another extended family will not mix with yours. They can use pretty much all the same nicknames without confusion. Thus, two men who know each other in the bazaar as Sayd Ahmed and Mohd Musa may both be Sher Kaka, or "Lion Uncle," at home. They probably won't know it though. People rarely mention their family nicknames in public. In Kabul, young people consider laqubs old-fashioned and claim not to have any.

A Crowded Place

Each compound in your village is likely to be a rather crowded place. In addition to your parents and siblings, for example, your grandparents may be living with you. Perhaps your father's brother and his whole family live in your compound as well. Perhaps a granduncle, an aunt, or an unmarried adult cousin lives here, too. The population of your compound depends on the situation of your whole family. It depends on who among your relatives need places to live.

As a child, you may often find yourself running errands for your elders. Afghans expect kids to help with household chores from an early age, and older people get to tell younger people what to do; that is the rule in an Afghan family. Furthermore, unless the age difference is very great, boys usually have more say than girls. The eldest son in a family may rule over his younger siblings almost like a father.

Afghan children accept the authority of elders, knowing that their own turn will come. If they live long enough, they will earn that highest badge of respect: white hair. Then they will be the ones to lounge about, fingering their prayer beads and telling stories. A dozen youngsters will leap to fulfill their faintest wish.

As an Afghan child, you probably don't have your own room, bookshelf, or closet. You don't have many toys. You have no place in the compound where you can close a door to shut out your family. You have no place to be alone with your thoughts and the things you own. But you don't miss these things. Afghans rarely want to be alone, and they would rather spend their time with people than with things.

As a result, Afghans spend a lot of time just keeping one another company. They do a lot of visiting. When you go to visit your cousin on the other side of the city, you feel no great need to get home that night. After all, you don't have much in your home compound that you don't have at your cousin's place. In both places you feel at ease because you are "among your own." So when Afghans visit relatives, the host usually begs them to stay the night, and the guests often accept.

Relatives can visit you, of course, as easily as you can visit them. And they can drop in suddenly, with no

The elderly are greatly respected in Afghanistan.

advance notice. In fact, it would be rude of them to give your family any such notice. Advance notice would mean they expect a big feast waiting for them when they arrive. Polite people, therefore, don't arrange to visit, they just arrive. If they have come far, their visit might last for days. If they have come from another town or village, they might stay for months. After three days, however, guests become ordinary members of the household. They have to pitch in with chores and fall in with the normal schedule of the household.

Dinnertime in the Compound

Women normally do the cooking for the household. When a meal is ready, they send the youngest children out to spread the word. Someone spreads a tablecloth on the floor and sets the food on it. If guests are present, men and women may eat separately. If it's just the family, everyone sits down around the same cloth. Someone— usually a child—goes around with a pot of water and a bowl. The child pours the water so that each person can wash his or her hands. Every Afghan family has a special pot-and-bowl set for this purpose called an *aftawa-lagan*. Washing hands before a meal is especially important in rural Afghanistan, because people eat with their hands. Also, there Afghans share food from a common platter instead of dishing it into separate plates. Eating with the hands is harder than it may sound. Learning to do so politely takes as much practice as using silverware.

After the meal one of the kids brings the aftawa-lagan around again. The platters, food, and tablecloth are cleared away. People sit and relax with their fruit and tea.

Probably the most common main meal consists of bread and soup followed by fruit and tea. When guests are present, however, the family may dip into some fancier recipes. Here are some of the dishes an Afghan family might cook. Be sure to have an adult help you, if you try out any of these recipes.

Quabuli Dumpukht (Baked Rice with Carrots and Raisins)

1/2 tsp. each: cinnamon, cloves, cumin, and powdered cardamom
1 medium red onion, chopped
1/2 cup plus 1 cup oil
1 lb. lamb, cut into 1-inch cubes
2 cups plus 1 cup water
1 tsp. plus 2 tsp. salt
2 medium carrots, cut into thin sticks
1 tsp. sugar
1 cup seedless black raisins
2 cups white rice (uncooked)

☛Grind spices (cinnamon, cloves, cumin, and cardamom) to make a mixture. ☛Fry chopped red onion in 1/2 cup oil, stirring often. ☞Add lamb, 2 cups water, 1 tsp. salt and spice mixture. ☞Cover and simmer about twenty minutes until lamb is tender. Remove the meat and save the liquid. ☞Fry carrots in 1 cup oil and 1 tsp. sugar. Remove carrots and drain. ☞Add raisins to oil and fry until they swell. ☞Remove and add to the carrots to drain. Save oil. ☞Add 2 tsp. salt and 1 cup water to meat juice. ☞Stir in rice and boil approximately 10 to 15 minutes, until the rice has lost its hard center. ☞Add the oil from carrots and raisins to the rice and mix well. ☞Place meat into large casserole and pour rice and juice over it. ☞Make a pocket in the rice and add raisins and carrots. ☞Cover and bake in a 350° oven for 30 minutes. ☞Remove and place meat on platter with rice over the meat. ☞Sprinkle carrots and raisins over rice. Serves 6.

Burauni (Eggplant with Meat and Tomato Sauce)

2 large eggplants, peeled and cut into 1/2-inch thick slices
1/2 cup oil
1 medium red onion, chopped
1/2 lb. ground beef
1 lb. diced tomatoes
1 8-oz. can tomato sauce
salt and pepper
1 cup yogurt
1/2 lb. feta cheese
2 cloves minced garlic

☞Fry the eggplant in oil until golden brown. Remove eggplant and discard all but one tablespoon of the oil. ☞Place eggplant in a warm place, such as a 300° oven. ☞Fry the onion until wilted. ☞Add ground beef and fry until brown. ☞Add diced tomatoes and tomato sauce and simmer for 20 minutes. ☞Add salt and pepper to taste. ☞In a blender, combine yogurt and feta cheese. Blend well. ☞Add some salt and ground garlic. Blend well. ☞In a baking dish, arrange eggplant slices on bottom of dish, spread some meat and tomato sauce over eggplant. Keep alternating layers of eggplant and sauce until there is no more eggplant left. ☞Spread the yogurt/cheese mixture over top. ☞Sprinkle with mint and serve with Quabuli Dumpukht. Serves 6.

Note: The yogurt/cheese mixture is a good substitute for *q'root*, a sauce that Afghans make from dried yogurt curd.

Firni (Cornstarch Pudding)

1/4 cup almonds
1/2 cup plus 2 cups cold milk
1/4 cup cornstarch
1 cup sugar
1/4 cup ground cardamom
1/4 tsp. saffron
1/2 cup unsalted pistachio nuts

☛Blanch the almonds by dipping them first into boiling water, then into ice water (A good idea is to place the almonds in a sieve.) ☛Peel and chop the almonds.
☛Stir cornstarch into 1/2 cup milk to make a thick paste. Stir cornstarch-milk mixture into 2 cups milk. ☛Add almonds, sugar, cardamom, and saffron. Mix well. ☛Cook over low heat until thick and clear—about 2 minutes. ☛Sprinkle pistachios in a pattern over the pudding. Serves 6.

7. *The Struggle for Education*

Somewhere in a small Afghan village a group of boys are sorting bullets in the alley between their compounds. Then one of them glances at the sun. All the boys stop what they are doing: The time has come. Guns clanking, they start across the village. They are headed to the mosque for their day's studies with the mullah.

For many centuries, mullahs were the only teachers in Afghanistan. A mullah is a Muslim religious figure: a man who knows Islam thoroughly and can lead group prayers. The mullah performs the rituals required by Islam at weddings, funerals, and other such events. Every community has at least one or two mullahs. In a small village and among nomadic bands, he may be the only person who can read and write.

Reading, Writing, and Religion

A mullah concentrates on teaching reading, writing, and religion. Usually, all his students are boys. In the countryside and villages of Afghanistan—where mullahs run the few schools that do exist—girls are expected to learn religion at home from their families. They are rarely expected to learn reading and writing at all.

A mullah's school, or *madrassa*, has always been rather informal. For one thing, he only teaches when he and his students have no other crucial work. In the past, farming duties came before study. Today, war is the great interruption. The mullah uses the mosque as a classroom, but on a sunny day he may move the class outdoors. School probably only lasts a few hours a day, since the mullah has many duties. No bell rings to mark the start of classes: The students simply gather when they know it's time. And although the mullah may be demanding, he does not give grades or hand out report cards. He is much like a personal tutor to his boys.

Religion lies at the core of all the mullah's teaching. Students learn to read so they can read the Koran, the holy book of Islam. This book is written in ancient Arabic, which uses the same letters as Dari and Pushto. By learning to read the Koran, children learn to read their own language as well.

Students of the mullah not only learn to read the Koran but to recite it aloud in a special, melodic, chanting way called *qira'ut*. This technique is used only to read the Koran, no other text. Experts at qira'ut read the Koran at special, solemn occasions such as funerals. The mullah may also teach boys to create calligraphy. Calligraphy is fancy handwriting that is meant to look beautiful. It is often used to copy out verses from the Koran.

Boys learn the basics of Islam from their parents and

A mullah teaches boys to read.

This boy is learning to write.

other relatives. The mullah teaches them the details and the fine points. He explains, for example, what Islam has to say about food, clothes, marriage, and the roles of men and women. He tells stories from the life of the Prophet that teach subtle lessons about proper conduct.

Today, however, one aspect of Islam that a mullah usually emphasizes the most is the idea of *jihad*. Jihad is any action taken to defend Islam. If defending the religion means fighting, then Muslims are supposed to fight. Killing in such a war is not a sin. Dying in such a cause makes a person a martyr and assures him (or her) of going to heaven. The Mujahideen believe their war against the government of Kabul is a jihad. (In fact, *Mujahideen* means "those who fight jihad.") In teaching boys about jihad, mullahs prepare boys for this war.

Competition for the Mullahs

About a hundred years ago, the government began building schools of another kind. These competed with the mullah schools of the day. Slowly, the government schools crowded the mullahs out of education. By 1979, when the war started, only nomads and people of the deep countryside studied with mullahs. The war has changed the balance back again. In rebel-run areas—which includes most of the countryside—children who go to school at all study with mullahs. In the cities and large towns, however, children still go to government schools.

The war, however, has damaged or destroyed many of the government schools. Most of these were village schools, destroyed by Soviet and Kabul government bombing. In 1977, one year before the Communists took power in Kabul, Afghanistan had 3,704 schools, about 977,000 students, and about 83,500 teachers. Today, only 350 government schools remain open. Only about 2,000 teachers work in these schools—and they teach nearly 400,000 Afghan children.

In areas run by the government, both girls and boys

go to school. In fact, because the government has drafted high school boys, there may be more girls than boys in these schools. Girls, however, go to separate schools, and they obey a dress code. They wear dark dresses, dark stockings, and white scarves. Boys can dress any way they like but are generally expected to dress neatly. In the younger grades, each day may start with a "clean-hands" inspection. The students line up in the courtyard. The head teacher or the principal walks along and examines their hands, fingers, and fingernails. Students with dirt under their fingernails can expect a rap across the palm with a whiplike poplar branch.

The government schools teach the same subjects as the mullahs and many more as well. Even with the Communists in power, government schools teach Koranic reading, religion, and calligraphy. But they also teach Pushto, Dari, geography, history, drawing, science, and mathematics. Children have to start studying a foreign language in fifth or sixth grade. Today, Russian is the foreign language emphasized in government schools.

As students move from grade to grade, they study more and more subjects. By seventh grade, they have about eighteen subjects a year. After seventh grade, students take the same subjects every year until they graduate. These include, for example, biology, chemistry, and physics. The Communists, however, have added subjects such as Communism, politics, and the history of

Afghanistan's ruling party to the curriculum. They have replaced the old textbooks written by Afghans with new ones translated from Russian. These are the same books used in Soviet schools. In the years from 1980 to 1989, the government sent about 130,000 children to school in the Soviet Union. At least some of these students, it seems, were trained to work as spies and terrorists among the Mujahideen.

A School Day in Kabul

In a government school, students must be obedient and polite. The very look of a classroom emphasizes the importance of discipline. Desks and chairs are set up in straight rows and columns. Students must stay in their assigned seats and cannot wander around the classroom for any reason. The teacher never, for example, invites students to work together in small groups. The whole class must pay attention at all times to the teacher up front.

In a boys' elementary classroom, every class has a student *kiftan* ("captain") who helps the teacher keep order. The captain is allowed to roam the aisles for this purpose and to carry a stick—a branch cut from a poplar tree. In theory, the student with the best grades gets to be captain. In practice, the best student may not have what it takes to deal with rowdy classmates. In such a case, a

bigger, stronger boy becomes the acting captain, even
though he may have lower grades. The captain keeps
order after one teacher leaves and before the next one
arrives. When a teacher enters the classroom, the whole
class stands, the way people do in a courtroom when the
judge walks in. They must remain standing until the
teacher gives them permission to sit. Like American
students of two centuries ago, Afghan students learn by
reciting—that is, by repeating what the teacher says. This
method is used in both government and mullah schools.
A first or second grade arithmetic lesson, for example,
might go like this: The teacher writes the multiplication
table for the number *four* on the board. Then he points to
the first item with a long stick and calls out, "One times
four is four." All the students repeat in a chorus, "One
times four is four." He points to the second item and cries,
"Two times four is eight." All the students repeat, "Two
times four is eight." He continues in this way until he and
his students have recited the whole table aloud several
times. The next day, he may call on individual students
to stand up and recite the table from memory.

By fifth or sixth grade, students have to write essays
from time to time. The teacher assigns topics such as
"Springtime," "Our Country," or "In Praise of Our
Leader." Good students are expected to use fine language and witty phrases. They pepper their papers with
lines from ancient and modern poets. They may toss in

Students and teachers in the courtyard of a provincial school.

a bit of their own poetry. Students are never required to go to a library, do research, or come up with new ideas for writing assignments. Unlike American students, few—if any—Afghan students have access to a library or to books other than the ones they get in school.

Walking into a typical Afghan classroom, you might see a map or two hanging on the wall. But you won't find any posters, student art, or bulletin board displays, as you will in most American classrooms. You won't find someone's science experiment laid out on a table. Nor will you see bookshelves, extra books, a supply cabinet, a reading corner, or a computer. The Afghan classroom is a bare room with little or no extra furniture.

At recess, students play in the school courtyard, unless there is a battle going on in the area. Then they may have to stay inside until the rocket fire stops. The courtyard may have a few bushes, but it has no playground equipment. Students play makeshift games or just sit and talk with friends.

Exam Days

Several times a year, all the students in a school—and, in fact, all the students in a whole city—take exams. These exams go on for days, since students have many subjects. In each subject, students take both a written and an oral exam. For the oral exam, they go one by one into a room to be questioned by the teacher. If their luck is running low, the school principal and even a government official may be present. The adults take turns posing questions, which the student tries to answer. Students' grades are based on their exams. Nothing else they do in the classroom counts. At the end of the year, their grades in all exams are added up. Those who pass go on. Those who fail repeat the grade. Repeating a grade is not uncommon for Afghan students.

After graduating from a government high school, students may apply to Kabul University. This school was founded in 1932. It had eleven colleges when the war started. Since then, however, the university has been closed more often than it has been open because of demonstrations, fighting, and other problems. Perhaps the most serious problem is that more than half of the professors have been jailed or executed, or have fled the country.

In rebel-controlled areas, American advisors from the University of Nebraska are now working to found yet another set of schools. They work with the local mullahs from each area, and so their schools only admit male students. The subjects taught in these schools, however, go beyond the reading, writing, and religion taught in the old-fashioned madrassas. The teachers are young men trained outside the country. This project claims to have planted about 1,200 schools across the countryside.

Meanwhile, in the refugee camps in Pakistan, the United Nations also runs a number of schools for Afghans. These include some two hundred schools for girls. Girls' schools, however, face a constant struggle for survival. That's because some (though not all) of the Islamic parties powerful among the refugees oppose education for girls.

In America, most schools teach roughly the same skills and the same subjects in the same general way. Afghanistan, however, is a bitterly divided country. Afghan schools reflect the split. In this country, schools are part of the war, part of the struggle for the minds and hearts of the people. The government schools try to shape students into willing citizens of a Communist state. In areas run by the Mujahideen, schools train students to be devout Muslims and prepare them for battle with the Kabul government. On both sides of the struggle, bombs and bullets often interrupt reading, writing, and arithmetic. What will school be like when Afghanistan is once again at peace? That is a question that nobody can answer today — peace seems too far away and the shape of it remains too unknown.

8. Games and Sports

Many children in Afghanistan have never known a time without war. The fact shows in their games and toys. Six-year-olds carry wooden machine guns. Boys set up battle scenes with homemade tanks. All this is new, for war games were never part of Afghan culture in the past. And even now, Afghan children still play the many games their grandparents played long ago in times of peace.

If you were to join the girls, you would probably recognize many of these games. Only the names would be strange to you. For example, the girls might invite you to join them in a round of *juz bazi*, out in the courtyard. Once you see the pattern of squares drawn in the dust you'll recognize juz bazi as a kind of hopscotch.

Hiding in Cracks and Corners

In the cracks and corners of a large compound, girls may play *chishm putukan,* or "little-eye-hiding." You probably call the same game "hide-and-seek." Afghan children shout "Mah!" when they spot someone hiding or when they get back to base unseen. Younger boys living in a compound may join the girls at chishm putukan. Older girls often find themselves taking care of babies. Like

people all over the world, they play a game that involves hiding from the baby. Then they pop up, uttering a word to amaze and delight the baby. Here in America the word is "Peekaboo!" In Afghanistan the word is "*Ti!*" (pronounced like "tight," but without the second *t*.)

An Afghan mother may use a yarrow bush as a broom, but her daughter sees the same bush as the basis for a doll. The yarrow bush has long, thin stalks. When tied together at the top, these stalks spread out at the bottom like a dress. Girls wrap a patch of cloth over the top for a head and embroider eyes and a mouth on it.

When the family cooks a chicken for dinner, the girls may ask for the wishbone, but not to make a wish. They want the bone so they can play *mara-yadast-tura-furamosh* (I remembered, you forgot). Two girls break the wishbone and each one takes half. From then on, each girl tries to trick the other into looking at her half. For example, one girl may hide the bone in a bit of cloth, wrap the cloth around her finger, and pretend she has been hurt. When her rival unwraps the cloth to see the injury—oh no: There's the bone. At that moment the girl sings out triumphantly, "I remembered, you forgot!" One sighting of the wishbone does not end the game. In fact the game can go on for days, until neither player is able to think of much else besides those pesky pieces of wishbone.

Some games don't have winners and losers. Among the Hazaras, for example, girls play a game called

Children's toys reflect the fact that war is a part of everyday life in Afghanistan. This boy plays with his homemade tank, built partially of bullet casings.

akhamchai. The girls crouch in a circle. Then they jump up and down in a pattern, making musical noises. It is as much a dance as a game.

Knucklebones and Ball Games

Boys gather in bunches to compete at *bujul-bazi*, a game played with the knucklebones of sheep. These bones are shaped like small, lumpy matchboxes. When rolled across the ground, they can either land upright or on their sides. The players take turns tossing several sheep knuckles at a time onto the ground the way people roll dice. The outcome of the game depends on how many of the knucklebones land upright and how many end up on their sides. Usually the players in bujul-bazi place bets. Since gambling is against the rules of Islam, many families disapprove of the game. Marbles are another popular "alley game" and are considered more respectable than knucklebones.

Older boys play all kinds of ball games. In common with most of the world, for example, Afghan boys enjoy soccer—which they, like most of the world, call *futball.* Of course they prefer to use a real soccer ball or even a tennis ball, if they can get one, but usually they can't. So then they make do with a homemade cloth ball stuffed with rags. Usually they use stones, hats, or coats to mark goalposts in an alley or an open field.

With a cloth ball and a stick, they can also play *top danda*. In this game a boy standing on one "base" pitches a ball to a boy standing on another base. The second boy tries to hit the ball with a board or a stick. If he connects and sends the ball flying, he runs back and forth between the two bases as many times as he can before the pitcher gets the ball back and tags him out. The ball used in this game often contains a rock to give it weight, so the batter can sometimes send it a long distance. Top danda resembles the game of cricket, which is popular in India and Pakistan as well as Britain.

Eggs and Larks and Flying Dolls

Some boys compete fiercely at *tukh'm-jangee,* or "egg fighting." In these contests, each player has a hard-boiled egg. One boy holds his egg in his fist, leaving just the tip of it exposed. The other boy slams his own egg down against that exposed tip. The player whose egg cracks loses the contest.

You might think that luck would decide the winner and loser in such a contest. Luck, however, seldom plays a role. Boys have countless tricks for strengthening the shells of their eggs. Some boys fill their eggs with something as hard and heavy as cement. What this stuff is and how the boys get it into the egg, I can't tell you—and I wouldn't, even if I knew, for each egg fighter has his own secret recipes and techniques. The game is really between these recipes and techniques. Wise egg fighters, therefore, do not lightly reveal their secrets.

As boys grow up, they may graduate from egg fighting to bird fighting. Roosters, partridges, and larks are all used as fighting birds. A contest between two fighting birds can draw a huge crowd in a bazaar. Spectators place bets as the birds face off. Bird fights—especially the ones between roosters—can be quite gruesome: The birds fight until one is killed.

A gentler game played with birds is called *kuftar-bazi,* or "pigeon play." In the game of pigeon play, boys and young men acquire flocks of pigeons and train them to fly out over the city and then come back home. When flocks of homing pigeons cross each other's paths, one or two pigeons usually get confused, especially if they have not been well trained. These pigeons return to the wrong roost. Ah, what triumph their new owner feels—for he has scored points in the game of "pigeon play." He has tricked away some other fellow's pigeons while proving the unshakable loyalty of his own! And that is what pigeon play is all about.

Another popular Afghan sport involves flight and fight of a different kind. *Gudi-paran jungi* actually means "flying-doll fighting." The flying dolls in this case are kites. The sport of Afghan kite fighting calls for physical and technical skill as well as competitive fire.

A boy with his pigeons, used in the gentle, fun game of pigeon play.

Over the centuries, Afghans, especially the boys of Kabul, have honed kite flying and kite fighting into a high art.

Friday has always been a favorite day for kite fighting because this is a holiday for Muslims, much as Sunday is for Christians. Good Muslims say their prayers five times every day, but on Friday, they make a social event of it, gathering at the mosque as recommended by the Prophet Muhammad. Afterward, most folks go home to relax, visit with friends, drink tea, play chess, or just lounge around. Dedicated kite fighters, however, climb to the roof or head to an open field with the tools of their sport.

Their main piece of equipment, of course, is their kite. This they probably made the night before, for no one buys a kite. Everybody makes his own by stretching thin tissue paper over a cross-frame of bamboo sticks. The finished kites have a diamondlike shape with two short sides and two long ones. Over the main kite, the kite maker pastes one or more smaller sheets of paper cut into interesting and flowery shapes. The second sheet (or sheets), which is of a different color (or colors), gives the kite a decorative look. Usually, this decoration vaguely resembles a face. Perhaps that is why kites are called "flying dolls." Since a good kite fighter needs a good kite, the best kite fighters are excellent kite makers as well. But a good kite alone does not ensure success. Kite fighters have to know how to maneuver their kites, making them swoop here and there like World War II airplanes in a dog fight. After all, the sport is not called flying-doll fighting for nothing. The whole point is to cross strings with another flyer, saw back and forth to break his string, and thus cut his kite loose.

Just as skilled fishermen can "read" the currents underwater by the feel of the line, kite-fighting boys can "read" the invisible currents of wind high above their rooftops. They can read it by the way the string feels, tugging and slipping through their fingers. They know just when to feed the string out, just when to haul it in again.

Smart boys also "glass" their strings for insurance. That is, they soak the string in a mixture of ground glass and paste. Once the string dries, it bristles with a jagged texture. No ordinary string can stand up to a glassed string in a kite fight. But then, among top kite fighters, ordinary string is about as common as lips on a chicken. Again, as with egg fighting, each boy has his own secret recipe for string-glassing and he guards his recipe with jealous care.

A losing kite—one whose string has been cut—goes floating away, of course. No one knows where it will land. The owner has little hope of recovering it. Younger boys who have no kites of their own go racing through the alleys, trying to calculate where the kite will land so they can claim it. Some run along the tops of walls or jump

A buzkashi *game in progress.*

from rooftop to rooftop in a nimble and dangerous dash. You might call this wall-and-rooftop running a second sport related to kite flying.

Buzkashi—the Sport of Warriors

The most distinctive Afghan sport is *buzkashi,* or "goat pulling." It is not a game for children—or even for most adults. The players, riding on horses, compete to carry the carcass of a goat or, more commonly, a calf from one end of a field to the other and back again. The field can be anywhere from a few hundred yards to many miles long. People sometimes play as teams and sometimes as individuals. The number of players in a game can vary from dozens to hundreds.

The calf starts out in a circle at one end of the field. At a signal, all the riders bear down and try to grab it up. They lean down, holding onto their horses with their legs. Whoever succeeds in grabbing and lifting the calf races for the other end of the field. The other players ride alongside, trying to snatch the prize away. Buzkashi has few rules and no referee. Players carry whips and use them freely. Those who get pulled off their horses sometimes get seriously injured.

The nomadic warriors of the northern plains invented this buzkashi and remain the masters of it. In the old days, before the war, big landowners and lords of the north kept stables of fine horses and sponsored their own expert *chapandaz*, as buzkashi players are called. Each chapandaz played not only for his own glory and his family's but for the honor and glory of his sponsor. The northern provinces sent their best teams to Kabul on national holidays to play in major buzkashi tournaments. Due to the war, the government no longer sponsors such matches. The game remains popular, however. It is now played in the refugee camps of Pakistan as well as in Afghanistan.

9. Afghans in America

Waheed Asim could not speak any English when he arrived in America, and he had never heard of pizza. Nonetheless, the teenager needed a job to help support his family, so he walked into a pizza parlor. With help from a friend, he filled out an application. Today this refugee from Afghanistan is a star in a peculiar American competition. He is the four-time national pizza-making champion. He won his medals in the pizza-making speed competition run by Domino's Pizza. Asim can knock out sixteen pizzas in two minutes and forty-five seconds. His pizza-making skill has won him $15,000 and two sports cars. On a ten-city tour of the United States, he went head to head with the local champion of each city and beat them all.

A Growing Group of New Americans

Asim is one of a growing group of new Americans: immigrants from Afghanistan. The group has only a short history. The first Afghans arrived in the United States less than a century ago. Even then, for fifty or sixty years, only a handful trickled over to settle here. One of this tiny handful was a man named Yosuf Dollha Joffrey. Joffrey

Waheed Asim speedily making pizzas at Domino's.

left Afghanistan in the 1920s and settled in Seattle, where he married Mary Galetti, an Italian immigrant. In 1930, Joseph and Mary Joffrey had a son, whom they named Anver Bey Abdullah Jaffa Khan. At school, however, the boy took on the "American name" Robert.

Joseph Joffrey's son Robert became a dancer and choreographer. In fact, he founded one of America's premier dance companies, the Joffrey Ballet. Almost from the start, critics saw the company as a rising force in American dance. By 1989, when Robert Joffrey died, his company was the third largest in America and one of the finest in the world.

Joseph Joffrey was an exception to a rule. In his day, Afghans rarely settled in the United States. They came only to study and go home. As late as 1977, almost all the Afghans in America were students. In that year, about three thousand Afghans were enrolled in American colleges and universities. Many of them were sent here by the Afghan government. Some, however, had struggled over on their own: A degree from an American school often meant a good government job at home.

Then came the great disaster—the war. Many Afghan students canceled their plans to return home. They changed from visiting foreigners to immigrants. These first immigrants found jobs and waited anxiously for news of their families. By and by, some of their relatives escaped to Pakistan by walking across the mountains of

Afghanistan dressed as nomads. Their relatives in America sent money to help them. The ones in Pakistan, in turn, sent what they could into Afghanistan to help more family members escape. Each extended family became like a bucket brigade, working to gather its members in one place again—America. Nowadays, therefore, if you see one Afghan in America, you can safely bet that at least some others of the same clan live nearby, or soon will.

Afghan Immigrants Today

About fifty thousand Afghans currently live in America and several hundred more are trickling in each year. The largest groups are in New York, Washington, D.C., Denver, the San Francisco Bay area, and Los Angeles. Substantial Afghan communities also exist in Portland, Oregon, and other midsized Western cities. When these refugees first arrived, many of them spoke constantly of going home again. That kind of talk has faded over the years. By and large, Afghan refugees now in America are planning to stay. Many have applied for citizenship or have already become American citizens.

These new refugees represent a thin slice of Afghan society. Virtually none, for example, were peasants back home. Almost all came from big cities. Many belong to prosperous or upper-class families. They include politicians and officials from various Afghan governments of the past thirty years.

In their native country, some of these Afghan refugees were well known intellectuals—poets, professors, and artists. One such luminous exile is Ustad Humayun Etemadi. Now in his seventies, this graceful gentleman served for thirty years as court painter and keeper of the Royal Afghan Library. All the books in his care were hand-lettered and hand-illustrated artistic treasures. He restored the old manuscripts and created new books. A master of miniature painting, he plied his art for an audience of two—the king and the ages. Hardly anyone else had a chance to see his work in Afghanistan. Now most of his paintings are in the Soviet Union's Hermitage Museum, along with the rest of the Royal Afghan Library. Mr. Etemadi himself lives in Alameda, California. He teaches classes sponsored by a group called the Afghan Cultural Assistance Foundation. About a dozen American students study the art of miniature painting with the old master. From time to time he exhibits the few pieces he has managed to save from a lifetime of painting—all he could carry with him when he left Afghanistan.

Starting Over

Not all Afghan refugees were famous or powerful, of course, but in coming to America many said good-bye to successful careers. They were teachers, lawyers, or bureaucrats. They were editors, judges, doctors, or even bankers. They could not speak English well enough to take up the same line of work in America. Or they simply couldn't find a use for their skills here; an Afghan law degree is just a piece of paper in America, since Afghan law is nothing like American law.

Akbar Nowroz, for example, used to teach high school chemistry in Afghanistan. He couldn't speak English very well, so teaching was out of the question when he moved to America. He always liked to draw, however, so he went back to school to learn technical drafting. His training in calligraphy helped him here, for it had given him a steady, precise hand. Like many refugees, he worked his way through school with night jobs. Today, he works in his new profession.

Other Afghans have started small businesses. They have opened stores selling rugs and other items imported from central Asia. Afghan restaurants have popped up in a number of major cities. One of the finest to date is the Helmand restaurant in San Francisco, which received a rave review in the national food magazine *Gourmet*.

Starting a business takes money, however. Most Afghans arrive on these shores without much money, even though they may have been well-to-do in Afghanistan. Usually, they have to start out in low-paying jobs that require no special skills. Only after saving their

money for years can they open a business. In this, they are no different from many other immigrant groups that have come to America.

Old Customs in a New Land

Most Afghan families in America try to live as they did in Afghanistan. Cousins and siblings get houses in the same area if they can. They visit back and forth as much as possible. Families get together at Eid and other holidays. They cook the food they were used to, substituting new ingredients as necessary. In areas where many Afghans live, stores have sprung up that stock such items as Afghan bread, q'root, and books written in Dari. In Fremont, California, so many Afghan children go to the schools that the school district has tried to hire special teacher's aides who speak Dari or Pushto.

But the patterns of Afghan life do not fit comfortably into American society. For example, in an Afghan family, authority is supposed to increase with age. But here, quite often, only the young people can make money, in various low-skill jobs. Therefore, they are forced to take charge of family affairs and make important decisions. They find they have to tell their elders what to do and this makes them feel guilty. On the other side of the coin, the older men of a family, unable to find work, sometimes feel useless and bitter.

The Helmand restaurant in San Francisco.

The situation for older women is even more difficult. Most of them cannot read or write or speak English. They have too much time and nothing to do. Back in Afghanistan, at this age, they would have been running a compound, sifting tribal gossip, arranging marriages, and entertaining visitors every day. Here the house is empty all day long: The men and women go to work and the children go to school. The young people arrange their own marriages and no one asks for Grandma's advice. No one comes to visit and they cannot go visiting, for everyone they know lives far away and they cannot drive. If they tried to take the bus, they would surely get lost.

Like other immigrants, Afghans have begun forming organizations to help each other through these hard times. For example, there is the Afghan Literacy Project in Contra Costa, California, run by a man named Sher Ahmad. He coordinates about one hundred volunteers to go into Afghan homes. These volunteers teach new refugees simple English and basic life skills such as counting change and reading signs. Recently, Sher Ahmad reports, one woman in the project got a driver's license. This may not sound like much. However, when this woman started out, a simple trip to the nearest store could turn into a nightmare. Unable to read signs, she had to find her way by looking for landmarks. Unable to read labels, she had to guess what the items on the shelves were from the pictures on the packages. If any problem cropped up with the cashier, she was really lost. In Afghanistan, this woman had rarely set foot outside one of her family's compounds. Getting a driver's license was not only a proud achievement, but a taste of amazing freedom.

Living in Two Worlds

In a family of Afghan immigrants, children have the easiest time. Those who were born in the United States or arrive here at an early age usually swim right into American society like fish into a lake. Ten-year-old Humayun, for example, quickly found the video game parlor in his new neighborhood. Of course, he had never seen such things in his life—they don't exist in Afghanistan—but he soon mastered a game called *Space Defenders*. In fact, he perfected the ability to win dozens of free games with a single quarter. Then he learned that he could sell off his free games to other kids for a dime apiece.

These children pick up English quickly. Pressed and encouraged by their families—who see in them their hope for the future—they tend to do well in school. But they also face the problem of living in two worlds. When they come home from school or the playground, they leave American culture behind and enter the world of their parents' culture—or at least, as much of it as the parents have been able to set up. The music they hear at home is likely to be Afghan or Indian music. The people they see socially are likely to be others of their own extended family. Teenagers are strongly discouraged from going on dates—even with other Afghans. The idea of marrying a non-Afghan would be unthinkable for most Afghan girls. Most Afghan boys, too, would prefer to marry an Afghan.

Parents and other elders try their best to get the children to speak Dari or Pushto. They look on the "Americanization" of the children with mixed feelings. On the one hand, they want the children to fit into American society and find success. On the other hand, they worry that their children will grow up to be strangers. They fear that the children will lose touch with their Afghan heritage and values.

In Arlington, Virginia, a suburb of Washington, D.C., a number of Afghans have started the Ariana School for Afghans to keep the Afghan heritage alive for their children. The school has half-a-dozen classes, divided into different age groups, and it produces its own books. About fifty children attend the school on Saturday mornings. The instructors are all volunteers and many are parents. They teach the children how to read and write Dari and Pushto, how to say their prayers correctly, and how to perform the other rituals of Afghan culture. They tell anecdotes from the Koran to illustrate moral lessons.

The children at the Ariana School also study the history and geography of Afghanistan. The school is growing, since this Virginia suburb has so many Afghan residents that Afghans call a part of it Deh Afghanan, or "Village of the Afghans."

Afghans are a new ingredient in the American melting pot. They will change the flavor of the stew in the years to come—and they will themselves be changed. No doubt some Afghans of American descent will make their mark, but in what field is impossible to predict. After all, who could have guessed that one of the first Americans of Afghan descent would excel in the field of ballet? Or that one of the latest would excel at making pizzas?

Appendix A

Afghan Embassy in the United States

Embassy of the Republic of Afghanistan
2341 Wyoming Avenue NW
Washington, D.C. 20008
(202) 234-3770

Appendix B

Pronunciation Guide for Afghan Names and Places

The following is a list of pronunciations to some Afghan names, words, and places. All other pronunciations appear in the glossary, which follows this appendix.

PEOPLE OF HISTORY, CULTURE, AND FOLKLORE

Ahmad Shah Masoud (UHH muhd shoy muh SOOD)
Ahmad Zahir (UHH muhd zaw HIR)
Aimaq (eye MUQ)
Amanullah (uh maw nu LAW)
Amir Abdu'Rahman (uh MEER uhb du raw MAWN)
Babrak Karmal (buhb RUHK kawr MUHL)
Babur (baw BUR)
Bachey Saqao (buh CHAY suh QOW)
Daoud (daw OOD)
Farsiwan (farsee WAWN)
Firdausi (fihr dow SEE)
Genghis Khan (chuhn KHAWN)
Hafizullah Amin (huh fee zu LAW uh MEEN)
Hafizullah Arbab (huh fee zu LAW uhr BAWB)
Hazaras (huhz aw RUH)
Hizbi Watan (hihzb ih wuh TUHN)
Humayun Etemadi (hu maw YOONI AI ti maw DEE)
Ibrahim (ib raw HEEM)
Ismail Khan (IHS maw eel KHAWN)
Khadi (khuh DEE)
Khalilullah Khalili (khuh lee luh LOY khuh lee LEE)
Kushan (ku SHAWN)
Leilah (ly LAW)
Majnun (muhj NOON)
Malalai (muh law LY)
Mohammadzai (maw muhd zuh EE)
Muhammad (mu HUHM uhd)
Mullah Nasruddin (mu law nuhs ru DEEN)
Murghalai (mur ghah LY)

Najibullah (nuh jee bu LAW)
Pushtoon (puhsh TOON)
Rakhsh (RAHKHSH)
Rustum (rus TUHM)
Subghatullah Mujaddedi (sub ghuht u LAW mu jah di DEE)
Sultan Mahmud (SUL tawn muhh MOOD)
Tajiks (taw JIHK)
Taraki (tuh ruh KEE)
Timur-i-lang (tay MUR ih LAHNG)
Turkoman (turk MUN)
Uzbek (uz BUHK)
Zahir Shah (zaw hihr SHAW)

TOWNS, REGIONS, AND GEOGRAPHICAL LANDMARKS
Afghanistan (uf GHAW nis tawn)
Baghlan (buhgh LAWN)
Balkh (BULKH)
Ghazni (ghuz NEE)
Gundumuk (guhn du MUHK)
Helmand (hehl MUND)
Herat (hay RAWT)
Hindu Kush (HIHN doo kush)
Kandahar (qun duh HAR)
Khyber (khy BUR)
Koh-i-Sherdarwaza (KOH ih shair dur waw ZUH)
Kohistan (koh ihs TAN)
Kunduz (qun DUZ)
Maiwand (my WUHND)
Masjidi Shahdu Shamshira (mahs JIDT ih shaw du shahm shay ruh)
Mazar-i-Sharif (muh ZAWR ih shuh REEF)
Nuristan (NOO ris tawn)
Pakistan (paw kis TAWN)
Panjsher (pahnj SHAIR)
Peshawar (pih shaw UR)
Pul-i-Khumri (PU lih khum REE)
Shiberghan (shi bihr GHAWN)
Wakhan (Waw KHAWN)

Glossary

aftawa lagan (UHF-taw-wuh luh-GUHN)—a matching pan and pot

akhamchai (uh-khum-CHY)—a game that involves jumping up and down in a rhythmic pattern

Allah (uhl-LAW)—the word for God in Arabic, used throughout the Holy Koran

Ariana (AW-ree-aw-NAW)—an early name for Afghanistan, based on the idea that the inhabitants were Aryans

armunia (ahr-mun-YUH)—a small hand-pumped organ

attan (uh-TUHN)—the folk dance of the Pushtoon, one of the main ethnic groups in Afghanistan

Austa Biro (aw-staw-bih-ROH)—"Go Slowly"—the traditional wedding song

Bachey Kul (buh-CHAY kuhl)— "The Bald Boy," a stock character in Afghan folk tales

Bactria (buhk-trih-AW)—another early name for Afghanistan, referring mainly to what is now northern Afghanistan

badal (buh-DUHL)—avenging blood for blood

beganas (bay-gaw-NUHZ)—outsiders to the family; strangers

Bood Nabood (BOOD nuh-bood)—"There was/there wasn't"—a phrase that is used to begin folk tales told in Dari

bujul-bazi (buh-juhl-baw-ZEE)—a game in which sheep's knuckles are used like dice

burauni (boh-raw-NEE)—fried eggplant with tomato sauce

buzkashi (buz-kuh-SHEE)—"goat pulling"—a game played on horseback in which players compete to grab a goat or calf carcass and carry it to a goal

chadri (chaw-duh-REE)— an ankle-length, baglike garment worn over the head by some Afghan women as a veil

chapandaz (chuhp-uhn-DAWZ)—a professional buzkashi player

chishm putukan (chih-shim pu-tuh-KAWN)—hide-and-seek

Dari (duh-REE)—a dialect of Persian and one of two main languages spoken in Afghanistan

Dohl (DOHL)—big drums

Eid-i-Qurban (EED-ih-qur-BAWN)—four-day holiday that marks the time when Muslims make the pilgrimage to Mecca if they can

Eid-i-Ramazan (EED-ih-ruh-muh-ZAWN)—three-day holiday that marks the end of the month of fast

Farsi (fawr-SEE)—one of the two main languages spoken in Afghanistan

firni (fihr-NEE)—cornstarch pudding with almonds and pistachios

ghayrat (ghy-RUHT)—courage; defense of property and manly honor

ghirghira (ghihr-ghih-RUH)—a wooden noisemaking toy often sold at New Year's Day fairs

gudi-paran jungi (guh-dee-puh-rawn juhn-GEE)—competitive kite flying

Haft Miwa (huhft may-WUH)— "Seven Fruits," a soup made from dried fruits and nuts and served on New Year's Day

Hajj (HUHJ)—the pilgrimage to Mecca, one of a Muslim's five main religious duties

inshallah (in-SHAW-law)—Arabic phrase meaning "if God wills it"—spoken whenever one announces a plan or intention

jelabi (ji-luh-BEE)—fried pretzel soaked in honey

jihad (jih-HAWD)—war fought in defense of Islam

Jinn (jihn)—one of a race of supernatural creatures which, Afghans believe, live invisibly among us and sometimes get inside of people

juz bazi (juhz baw-ZEE)—a kind of hopscotch

kahrez (kaw-RAIZ)—a series of connected wells, used to irrigate fields

Khalq (Khulq)—"The People"; one of two factions of the ruling Communist party in Afghanistan

Khorasan (khur-aw-SAHN)—an early name for Afghanistan as a province of the Persian Empire

Khudawand (khud-aw-WUHND)—the word for God in Persian. Afghans use both Allah and Khudawand to speak of the Supreme Being

kiftan (kihf-TAWN)—a boy who serves as "captain" or enforcer of order in a classroom

kochis (koh-CHEEZ)—nomadic herders, who have no fixed home but travel constantly

Koran (Qu-RAWN)—the sacred book of Islam, considered by Muslims to be the direct word of God

kuftar-bazi (kuhf-tuhr baw-ZEE)—the sport of keeping pigeons

lapis lazuli (LAP-is luh-ZOO-lee)—blue precious stone

laqub (luh-QUHB)—a family nickname

madrassa (muhd-ruh-SAH)—a traditional school, in which the teacher is a mullah

mara-yadast-tura-furamosh (MUH-ruh-YAW-duhst-TUH-ruh-fuh-raw-MOHSH)—name of a game; literally "I remembered, you forgot"

melmastia (mel-MUST-ih-uh)—being a warm and generous host

Mujahideen (mu-jaw-hih-DEEN)—"those who fight for Islam"; warriors in the resistance movement against Afghanistan's Communist government

mullah (mu-LAW)—a religious teacher and authority on the rules and traditions of Islam

naan (NAWN)—bread; also, food

namaaz (nuh-MAWZ)—ritual prayers said five times daily by followers of the religion of Islam

namus (naw-MOOS)—defending the honor of women

nanawati (nuh-naw-WUHT-ee)—the obligation to give asylum to one in need of it

Nowroz (now-ROHZ)—New Year's Day, March 21

Parcham (puhr-CHUHM)— "The Banner;" one of two factions of the ruling Communist party in Afghanistan

Pushto (push-TOH)—the language of the Pushtoons and one of two main languages spoken in Afghanistan

qala (quh-LAW)—a fortress-style country home

qaubuli dumpukht (qaw-bu-LEE duhm-PUKHT)—baked lamb with fried carrots and raisins

qira'ut (qih-raw-UHT)—a melodic method of chanting the Koran aloud

q'root (qu-ROOT)—a tangy white sauce made from dried yogurt curds and used in many Afghan dishes

Ramazan (ruh-muh-ZAWN)—a month during which Muslims fast from dawn to dusk

rebab (ruh-BAWB)—a stringed instrument with as many as 17 strings

sabat (suh-BAWT)—being steadfast

shirni-khuri (shihr-nee-khoh-REE)—"The candy eating;" an engagement party

surnai (suhr-NY)—a wind instrument with a high, weedling tone

tabla (tuh-blah)—a pair of small drums played by hand

talab-gari (tuh-luhb-gaw-REE)—a series of visits by members of a man's family to a woman's family; in these visits the man's family seeks the woman's hand in marriage

top danda (tohp duhn-DUH)—a kind of stickball

tukh'm jangi (tu-khum juhn-GEE)—a game in which hard-boiled eggs are knocked together to see which one breaks first

Selected Bibliography

Ahsan, M.M. *Muslim Festivals*. Vero Beach, Florida: Rourke Corp., 1987.

Clifford, Mary L. *The Land and People of Afghanistan*. Philadelphia: Lippincott Jr. Books, 1989.

Griffiths, J. *Conflict in Afghanistan*. Vero Beach, Florida: Rourke Corp.

Hood, Abdul Latif Al. *Islam*. New York: Franklin Watts, 1987.

Karim, F. *Heroes of Islam, Book Eight: Mahmood of Ghazni*. Chicago: Kazi Publications.

Miller, William M. *Tales of Persia: A Book for Children*. Phillipsburg, New Jersey, 1988.

Shah, Idries. *The Pleasantries of the Incredible Mulla Nasrudin.*Cambridge, Massachusetts: Octagon Press, 1983.

Shokla, Surinder K. *Afghanistan*. New York: Apt Books, 1989.

Index

About the Author

Mir Tamim Ansary was born in Afghanistan, where he grew up bilingual and bicultural. His father was among the earliest Afghan students in the United States. His mother was one of the first (half-dozen or so) American women to marry an Afghan and live in Afghanistan. After attending Istiqlal High School in Kabul, Mr. Ansary came to the United States to complete his studies. Later, he edited *The Asian Student* and other publications for The Asia Foundation in San Fran-

cisco. In 1979, Mr. Ansary traveled through the Muslim world. Upheaval in North Africa, revolution in Iran, and the Soviet invasion of Afghanistan cut his travels short. He returned to San Francisco, where he went to work as an editor for a major children's book publishing company. His articles and short fiction have appeared in publications ranging from *The Los Angeles Times* to *Prism International*.

Currently he lives in San Francisco with his wife, Debby, and his daughters Jessy and Elina, makes his living as a freelance writer, and is working on an epic novel about Afghanistan.